PSYCHO-PICTOGRAPHY:

The New Way To Use The Miracle Power Of Your Mind

Psycho-Pictography

The New Way To Use The Miracle Power Of Your Mind

VERNON HOWARD

Parker Publishing Company, Inc. West Nyack, New York

LIBRARY OF CONGRESS
CATALOG CARD NUMBER: 65-22193

Reward Edition . . . . . November, 1973

Tenth Printing . . . . . September, 1979

PRINTED IN THE UNITED STATES OF AMERICA

B & P

Other books by VERNON HOWARD

For list of books & tapes
by Vernon Howard write:
BOX 684
BOULDER CITY, NEVADA 89005

THE MYSTIC PATH TO COSMIC POWER

HOW THE DYNAMIC SCIENCE OF
PSYCHO-PICTOGRAPHY WORKS FOR YOU

Psycho-Pictography can change your life instantly—from the very moment you let it work for you.

Regardless of your circumstances or age or personal problems, this tested science carries you to the refreshing atmosphere of a sky-high life. Just as anyone can let an airplane carry him lightly aloft, so can you soar far above your burdens. Psycho-Pictography lifts you to undreamed of heights, where failure and misfortune are no longer in sight.

You may inquire, "Exactly what is Psycho-Pictography and how does it carry me aloft?"

You will find complete details about this wonder-science in Chapter 1, but let's now explore together a few helpful facts. *Psycho* indicates the mind, while *Pictography* is the use of pictures to convey an idea. So *Psycho-Pictography* is the use of Mental Pictures to convey spiritual and psychological truths that set a man free.

Psycho-Pictography is the science of absorbing Mental Pictures which provide the mind with powerful and accurate guidance. Once received into your mind *they work effortlessly* to uplift your entire life. You need not strain with them; they become your silently faithful servants who work for you day and night.

The wonderful new life you will find in this book has already been discovered by thousands of men and women. They used the principles of Psycho-Pictography, though they may not have called it by that name. You have the advantage of using the *first book* to organize and present Mental Pictures as a practical science for self-enrichment.

Psycho-Pictography is both an ancient wisdom and an up-to-date technique. It combines the time-honored universal truths with modern findings of psychology. The result is a thrilling system that *really works*. The science of Psycho-Pictography was developed by your author after many years of careful study and practice.

Your enrichment begins from the moment you absorb these Mental Pictures, but you must give them time to work for you. So stick with it, read and review, make this book your close companion for at least three weeks. Do your part as a persistent student of Psycho-Pictography. Then, you can be sure of that new stirring within that announces a transformed self.

You will find it easy and interesting to absorb the Mental Pictures. So relax as you read. A major secret of this science is to release your own struggling efforts and let yourself be carried lightly aloft.

Let's adventure forward together toward the wonderful new life.

Vernon Howard

VERNON HOWARD LIVES AND TEACHES IN BOULDER CITY. WRITE: NEW LIFE, BOX 684, BOULDER CITY, NEVADA 89005-0684

YOUR GUIDE TO MENTAL PICTURES

Here is how to enrich yourself with the 94 Mental Pictures in this book: Turn to the page indicated, where you will find a numbered Mental Picture. Start your reading a few paragraphs before the number, and continue for a few paragraphs after it. This supplies an introduction and a conclusion to the Mental Picture, giving it full meaning.

CONTENTS

The Miracle Method
of Psycho-Pictography

"I rarely admit it," my caller said, "but I am in despair over finding the truth that might set me free. Does it really exist? Can I find it? How?"

"The truth exists. It is a reality. It exists within you at this very moment. You may not be aware of it as yet, but still it is there. Your part is to listen when it speaks."

An illustrative story helped to clear the idea in the caller's mind:

A Swiss shepherd boy was kidnapped by passing gypsies. As he was hustled away inside the wagon, he heard the ringing of the village bell. The sound became fainter and fainter as the wagon carried him away. But that bell's special tone made a permanent impression upon his mind.

Years later, as he grew up, the memory of that bell stirred a restless urge within. It made him weary of the gypsy life. He longed to return to his rightful home. So he broke away from the gypsy camp and began his search. He wandered from country to country, village to village, listening intensely for the special ring of that single bell. He heard many peals as he journeyed along, but he always detected a false ring, and so refused to be lured away.

Finally, while pausing by the roadside to rest, he heard a faintly familiar peal. He turned in its direction. The farther he walked the more swiftly he stepped. Something within him *knew* that he was hearing his village bell at last. And he followed it all the way home.

Likewise, the ring of truth is inside every man. And this is not something merely mystical or philosophical. It is a practical fact. If a man learns to listen, if he refuses to be lured away by false sounds, he will find his way home. The ring of truth will always be recognized by the man who listens. And every man has the capacity to listen and to follow. [MENTAL PICTURE 1]

You, the reader, have just received your first Mental Picture from this book. There will be many more. But first we want to discover what we mean by Psycho-Pictography, the dynamic science of Mental Pictures.

The Miracle Method

Throughout the ages, a major challenge has confronted the great teachers of Truth. It had to be met by philosophers, psychologists, scientists, and teachers of religion. That challenge is: *By what method can the human mind be reached with the Truth that sets it free?*

Offhand, this would seem to be no problem at all. We might answer, "Why, just *tell* people about the bright new life they can have. They will respond eagerly enough!"

Yet, we know from tragic evidence that this is not so. Even a brief glance at the headlines reveals that men have lost the ability to respond to self-enrichment. The mind of man, far from welcoming advancement, resists it fiercely. The ego-centered self, fearing defeat at the hands of Truth, fights back with every weapon it can frantically grasp. The human mind, when faced with the very power that gives light and liberty, has invented a multitude of evasions, resistances, rationalizations, and counterfeits.

Faced with this challenge, the great teachers of history developed ways and means to carry the Truth beyond these mental barriers. They have discovered methods for giving a man his first magnificent glimpse that leads to his True Self.

Of all these techniques, only one was widely used at all.

And it was superbly successful.

It worked.

People took command of their own lives. Inner strength replaced weakness and fear. Problems unraveled. An entirely new self-identity appeared. Anger and anxiety turned to calm. Physical ailments vanished. Each new day, which formerly threatened another terror, now presented another conquest. Lives took on fresh meaning and permanent purpose.

Regardless of the human problem, no matter how disastrous or how long it had lasted, a healing took place. The technique proved all-powerful.

What was it?

The *Mental Picture.*

What Is a Mental Picture?

A Mental Picture is a scene played upon the screen of the mind. By means of a story or anecdote, the mind is helped to see a certain truth. For instance, we have just read the adventure of the Swiss shepherd. That story conveyed a picture to us. It impressed the intellect with a profound principle.

The value of Psycho-Pictography, or Mental Pictures, is enormous. We shall see how and why as we go along. For one thing, the thinking process itself is largely a projection of mental scenes. That is why constructive visualizations are essential to our health and happiness.

In this book you will be presented with many stories and illustrations that create positive Mental Pictures. These illustrations are the means by which the truth reaches and enlightens the mind. We can call these illustrations by various names—stories, examples, case-histories, analogies, anecdotes, even jokes. But the purpose is single: *to give the mind a constructive course of action to follow*. They guide the individual into doing what is necessary in order to emerge with a new life.

Say, for instance, that you have a difficult decision to make. As hard as you try, you cannot make up your mind. Then, you read an anecdote about someone in a similar situation. You discover how he handled it. Perhaps he gave up fighting his problem and simply relaxed from it. That action loosened his mental powers, enabling him to think in a new way. And the answer came to him.

This man's success formed a Mental Picture in your mind. And now you have a clear and practical course to follow.

We may not immediately understand a particular idea that can help us, but we *can* understand a Mental Picture that illustrates it. So the Picture becomes a sturdy bridge. It helps us to cross over from the known to the unknown. It connects one level of understanding to a higher level. We ascend from a literal understanding to a psychological insight.

The use of stories to convey a principle has another interesting advantage. Because they are pleasant to read, because we enjoy them, they permit passage of the truth with minimum of resistance. Stories are like friends who bring us unexpected gifts.

How Mental Pictures Work for You

An absorbed Mental Picture goes to work at once. It transforms our thinking. Like a powerful current beneath the surface of the sea, it supplies energy and wisdom, even when we are not consciously aware of it. Quietly it works, giving us whatever we need for a conquest.

This enormous secret was known and used by all the great teachers of history. The New Testament presented Mental Pictures by means of parables. Zen Buddhism did likewise with its anecdotes and analogies. Ancient wise men, like Socrates and Plato, taught with stories and legends. Moderns, like Emerson and Thoreau, made full use of illustrations in their lectures and writings.

Why? Because Mental Pictures speak a language that everyone understands. *All of us are capable of forming mental images and of drawing meaning from them.*

Dr. Raynor C. Johnson explains:

> *The great teachers . . . have therefore always entrusted Truth with most confidence to parables, which, because of their simplicity, picturesqueness and association with everyday life, are a thought-form most likely to be remembered and least likely to be corrupted. Each man, then . . . can*

perceive that depth of Truth to which he has a capacity to respond.[1]

All this is of thrilling significance. It means that anyone can start exactly where he is—regardless of his present knowledge or understanding—and go on to higher levels of fortune. A Mental Picture, once implanted, works ceaselessly and effortlessly. You have heard the ancient saying that a picture is worth a thousand words. We can modernize it by saying that a Mental Picture is worth a thousand hours of effort!

Let's review our discoveries about Psycho-Pictography:

1. We read a story or illustration or ancedote.
2. That story impresses a picture upon the mind about a successful course of action.
3. The Mental Picture becomes a permanent power that channels all our natural energies—emotions, desires, physical forces, and so on—into a similarly successful action.
4. We more and more develop the casual ability to succeed in our chosen areas.

How Soon Will Results Appear?

You may ask, "How soon can I expect practical results from using Mental Pictures?"

Results arrive at once. The very moment a person reads a basic principle for loftier living he experiences some kind of reaction to it. This reaction may be somewhat vague at first, but by sticking with it, a clearer recognition grows. Like looking into a mirror, you see who you are and what you can do with yourself. A typical remark of a person who is gaining more self-understanding is, "I'm not sure what is happening as yet, but it's definite and interesting."

Change is certain. At first it may be in small ways, for instance, you are less upset by an unkind remark from someone. Or maybe you see that it is not selfish to live your life as you see fit; it is selfish only to insist that others live as you see fit.

Life flows from the inner to the outer. Good changes you make

---

[1] Raynor C. Johnson, *The Imprisoned Splendour* (New York: Harper and Row, Publishers, Incorporated, 1953).

in the inner self will reflect favorably in your outer activities. You can actually *observe* these exterior improvements as they take place. Your business activities take on a fresh look; your relations with other people become smoother—as we shall see in later chapters. All this happens because your inner unity creates total power. A man with self-unity is like a river which was once divided by several islands but which finally flows together again beyond them.

Suppose it is seven o'clock and you want to catch a certain television program coming on at eight. You can tune your set to the correct channel *now*. Then, all you need do is wait for it to come to you. You can relax in the knowledge that you are correctly tuned in, that the program *must* eventually be yours to experience. You need have no care nor responsibility for its arrival. Finally, of its own accord, and at the right time, your desire appears. [MENTAL PICTURE 2]

Likewise, with rich results—as long as we are correctly tuned in, by using Mental Pictures, we need not concern ourselves at all with results. They arrive all by themselves, easily and naturally.

In my previous book, *SECRETS OF MENTAL MAGIC: How to Use Your Full Power of Mind,*[2] I introduced the Mental Magic Party. This is a study group of men and women who wish to find themselves. Groups were formed throughout the nation. Many of the problems and questions examined in this book came from such groups. The answers to these questions, and the results in practical life, are of value to you.

How Confusion Helps

At this point I want to discuss with you the problem of confusion. As you go through these pages, do not be afraid to be confused. *Confusion is an honest emotion.* A man has broken well into the open when he can say, "I don't know," without being

---

[2] Vernon Howard, *Secrets of Mental Magic* (Englewood Cliffs: Prentice-Hall, Inc., N.J., 1964).

afraid of what he has just said. To realize that you don't know this or that, is the beginning of new wisdom. For instance, it is not wrong to be puzzled about what you want from life, any more than it is wrong not to know what kind of food you want for dinner. It is never wrong to be either physically or psychologically hungry. What *is* wrong is to accept a piece of fruit without determining whether it is real or artificial.

Do not shy away from a new idea that appears beyond your understanding. No principle is beyond human understanding. It cannot be. The Truth, however veiled it may be at the present, already dwells within every man and woman.

You need not understand the mechanical workings of an airplane in order to be carried aloft. Neither need you wholly grasp the pleasant changes that will take place within you. Let them happen. Relax with your study of Psycho-Pictography. Do not strain at understanding anything. Read with a sense of curiosity and exploration. See everything as good news. Enjoy the adventure.

A story was written about a coastal village that was attacked time and again by great sea monsters. The villagers heard of a magician who could dissolve all kinds of evil simply by looking at it with his all-powerful gaze. Called to the village, he took a stand on a high cliff overlooking the sea. The next time the monsters appeared, he looked steadfastly at them—and they vanished forever. [MENTAL PICTURE 3]

Any man can become such a magician. If he will not be afraid of his own confusion, if he will continue to *look until he sees,* all his negativities will vanish forever.

Asked Martha B., "A curious thing happens as I make progress. I always get *more* confused just before I actually see a truth for the first time. Why is this?"

"You were really as confused as before. Only it was subconscious. You merely became more *aware* of your confusion; you brought it to the surface. You realized for the first time that you really didn't understand as much as you thought. This self-honesty led to genuine understanding—and relief."

Martha laughed, "Yes, I've noticed what a relief it is to stop pretending!"

The Reason Why You Can Be Happier

The reason why a man does not live happily is not because that state is non-existent. Also, it is not because happiness is unattainable. Furthermore, it is not because someone or something stands in his way.

The reason why a man fails to attain his rightful contentment is for a reason he rarely suspects.

I would like you to read the next few paragraphs with special care. If you will grasp them, even just a bit, you will make more progress in seconds than perhaps you have made in years.

A man fails to attain personal liberation because *he is unaware that such a state actually exists.*

A man never goes after something unless he at least suspects that it is real, that it is there. He must therefore become consciously aware—*even if dimly at first*—that an entirely new world exists for him.

This new world has been proclaimed throughout the ages to unthinking mankind. It appears when a man or woman becomes receptive to esoteric knowledge, secret knowledge. It is secret only because millions of unhappy people will not receive and do not understand it. But you, the reader, can dare to be different. Then you will be different from the millions of unhappy people. You will know the truth that sets you free.

You may be sure that we are not talking about anything remote or impractical. We are looking into a far superior way of life that you can find and enjoy *today.*

Man's most tormenting and most carefully concealed fear is that there is no alternative road to the one which he now painfully endures. There *is* an alternative—and an utterly peaceful one—but he must express a rebellious sort of courage in order to find it. He must deliberately abandon his so-called securities and start down a new road, as unfamiliar as it may be. By using the Four Golden Keys (provided later), he finally finds what he seeks.

A new life of abundant cheer is found in one way, and one way only. All others lead to endless anxiety.

It is found through an awareness of its existence.

This is the entire secret. We must catch a glimpse of this fresh life for ourselves. We can start by remembering that it exists within, not without. We already possess this higher state. But we must become *aware* of our rich possession. This awareness will break through, with increasing force, as we dare to seek it beyond our present mental attitudes.

What prevents us from being aware? Our own resistances. We are afraid that if we let go of our present beliefs—as useless as they are—that the unknown might be even worse. But we must dare. And then we find that the very thing we feared was our very liberty!

Suppose you tell a man that just over the hill there is a grand castle, ready for his occupancy. He will want to believe you, but will be unable to do so. He has been fooled too many times by too many people. All his previous journeys have led to disappointment. He is not going to risk getting hurt again. So you really can't blame him for balking.

Nevertheless, the castle actually exists, whether he ventures toward it or not. Claimed or not, it is always there, ready for him.

Here we seem to have a major problem. The man will not walk toward the castle until he sees it. Yet he cannot see it until he walks toward it.

No problem. There *is* a way out. And any man can take it.

You Must Take the First Step

Let's suppose that our man is willing to take the first hesitant step away from familiar ground, toward the castle he cannot see as yet. Suppose he willingly walks just far enough to catch his first glimpse of the castle. Maybe he sees only a tiny top corner. *That is enough!* He has seen something that makes him excited, curious, eager. Everything within him responds to that first grand glimpse with new vitality. So now he takes a few more forward steps, then some more, until he finally possesses the castle. It is his to occupy and enjoy. [MENTAL PICTURE 4]

Sometimes, during the course of an ordinary day, we catch brief glimpses of this new life. It usually comes with sudden delight. One instance was related by a class member:

"I was driving down the street feeling angrily aggressive. The morning had gone all wrong. My anger transferred itself to my driving. I felt like ploughing through traffic without regard for anyone. I came to an intersection at the same time as another driver. I was about to plunge ahead, my turn or not, when an amazing thing happened. The other driver smiled pleasantly and waved me on. Three blocks later it struck me like lightning. That man was living in an entirely different world than I! I was overwhelmed with the fantastic truth that *there is another way to live!*"

You will find, as you go along, that Mental Pictures help you catch your first glimpse of your own grand castle.

How to Use Operation Tossaway

How does an alert awareness solve daily difficulties? Let's take a familiar problem that was expressed by one man: "Doctors and psychologists declare that a man has all the natural energies he needs. If this is so, why are there so many tired people—including myself?"

The fable is told of the traveler staggering down the road with a rock in one hand and a brick in the other. On his back was a sack of earth, and around his waist was wound a long coil of vines. On his head was balanced a heavy pumpkin.

Along the way he met a villager who asked, "Weary traveler, why burden yourself with that big rock?"

"That's odd," replied the traveler, "but I never really noticed it before." So he tossed the rock aside and felt much better.

Along came another villager who inquired, "Tell me, weary traveler, why wear yourself out with that heavy pumpkin?"

"I'm glad you pointed it out," said the traveler, "because I didn't realize what I was doing to myself." So he knocked the pumpkin off his head and went on his way with a much lighter step.

One by one, the villagers made him aware of his needless burdens. So one by one, he abandoned them. Finally, he was a free man—and walked like one. [MENTAL PICTURE 5]

What, really, was his problem? The rock and the pumpkin? Not really. *It was his unawareness of them.* Once he *saw* them as pointless burdens, he dropped them soon enough and was no longer tired.

That is the daily problem of many people. They are carrying unnoticed loads. No wonder they are tired!

What are some of these loads that burden a man's mind and steal his energy? Negative thoughts. Blaming and accusing others. Permitting gloomy impressions to nap in our minds. Carrying a load of false guilt for things we couldn't help. Self-pity. Believing that there is no way out.

Everyone has his special brand of energy-robbing burdens. The sooner we start Operation Tossaway the sooner we will feel better and walk lighter.

This Is Your Secret for Achieving Happiness

This brings us to a vital truth that you will meet many times in this book: *Inner freedom is not a matter of adding anything —it is purely a ridding process.* Here is one of the most startling and rewarding ideas you could ever grasp.

Suppose you once had a path across a meadow, but one day found it overgrown with weeds. To restore it, you would not *create* anything, rather, you would remove something. As the shrubs and weeds are cleared away the path appears. So it is with the mind. We need not try to create anything, for there is nothing that needs to be created. Freedom is already present, though perhaps as yet unseen.

Our mental weeds are made up of negative imaginations, fearful attitudes, unrealistic ideas, an insistence that we already know the answers, and so on. As self-understanding removes them—as it always does—we see the path for the first time. That puts us on the forward march.

As simple as this idea is, it eludes us. Therefore, we must think about it, review it. We are in the habit of thinking in terms of building, adding, constructing; while all the time, our freedom lies in the opposite direction. Happiness is a *ridding* process.

In discussing various steps to freedom, Professor Edwin A. Burtt writes:

> *Next, we must clearly recognize that the way to truth and blessedness does not lie in creating anything that does*

not now exist, nor in acquiring anything that is not now at hand . . . We need only remove ignorance; insight into the truth then dawns.[8]

Your Four Golden Keys to New Freedom and Happiness

There are Four Golden Keys for discovering the True Self, the Self that is free and happy. They are:

1. A sincere desire for inner change
2. Contact with workable principles
3. Self-honesty
4. Persistence

1. A sincere desire for inner change: A man must really want to be different. His first desire should be for the Truth itself, not for ideas that please him by backing up what he already believes. The earnest man dares to sail uncharted seas. When he finally reaches port he finds that this New World, though strange at first, is what he really sought all along. "I should say sincerity, a deep, great, genuine sincerity, is the first characteristic of all men in any way heroic." (Thomas Carlyle)

2. Contact with workable principles: This means we must be in contact with some source of genuine help. It can be a person who has already set himself at liberty, it can be a book, or it can be our own matured way of thinking. We must beware of counterfeits; we must not accept something as true merely because it appeals to us. We must make every offered idea *prove* itself to be a workable principle, we must personally verify everything.

3. Self-honesty: Genuine courage consists in being honest with oneself. The really heroic person is willing to be wrong for the present in order to be right later on. But honesty does not mean that you change your viewpoints merely for the sake of change; it means you explore your viewpoints in order to separate truth from falsity. Then, truth dissolves falsity. There is nothing of more practical use than self-honesty.

4. Persistence: A person may be sincere, and he may have found a source of genuine help. And he may also have a full supply of

---

[8] Edwin A. Burtt, *Man Seeks the Divine* (New York: Harper and Row, Publishers, Incorporated, 1957).

self-honesty. By adding one more thing, he has all he needs for swift strides forward; it is that old-fashioned and admirable quality we call persistence. A man must keep going. As the New Testament phrases it, he must not fall by the wayside. Persistence pays.

Whenever someone tells me that his way is blocked by discouragement or confusion, I ask him to check over the **Four Golden Keys**. It's not long before he finds the barrier at his back, and himself on the open highway once more. You can do the same.

How to Use the Transfer Technique

In the business world Leonard E. had achieved money and prestige that was not matched by inner wealth. He had, however, arrived at that stage of honest inquiry where he asked, "What's wrong? I feel that the answer is nearby, but I just can't grasp it. How do I find this inner richness you speak about? If I could just catch a clue or two, I believe I could go on from there. What's the missing link?"

"Imagine yourself at your office desk. Suppose you become aware of something wrong in your business operations. For instance, let's say that your methods for attracting new customers are not working out. What would you do? Would you try to deceive yourself that all is well?"

"Not at all. It would be too costly."

"Then you'd face the realities of the situation, even if it means changing your viewpoints?"

"Of course. You can't make money by avoiding economic realities."

"You wouldn't resist a new program that looked good?"

"I'd investigate it with enthusiasm."

"How would you know that you were on the right track at last?"

"There's only one way—by actual results; when sales really increase; when the situation definitely changes from bad to good."

"How about persistence? How long would you continue to work with this new program?"

"All the time. All the way. I'd stick with a winner."

"All right, why not apply the same realistic principles to your inner life?"

"Sounds like a good idea."

"Learn to see the parallel between business success and personal happiness. It might sound strange at first, but both are based on the very same fundamentals—realism and honesty and persistence."

"And I'm not using those in my personal life? No, I guess not. Otherwise I'd have the results I want."

"Be utterly practical. Transfer these business principles to your inner life. Call it the Transfer Technique. You'll get results." [MENTAL PICTURE 6]

Leonard succeeded. He *couldn't* fail. And neither can anyone else who uses the Transfer Technique. Just find some area of everyday life where you have already succeeded, such as a talent for music. A close look will show that the **Four Golden Keys** made it possible. Now transfer them to an inner area where you want a new success, such as trying to understand yourself better. You will transfer your success also.

VALUABLE REVIEW OF CHAPTER 1

1. Remember the story of the Swiss shepherd.
2. Psycho-Pictography is a tested technique for giving fresh meaning and permanent purpose to your life
3. A Mental Picture is created in your mind by reading a story, illustration, or case-history.
4. You can start exactly where you are to benefit from the dynamic method of Psycho-Pictography.
5. Let results come naturally and effortlessly.
6. Study Psycho-Pictography with a relaxed mind.
7. Dare to take the first step toward your rightful castle.
8. Happiness comes as we toss away needless negatives.
9. Let the **Four Golden Keys** supply you with accurate guidance.
10. The Transfer Technique works wonders.

2

The One Way to Get
Something for Nothing

It is said that the best things in life are free. They are. That is why a man must stop trying to pay for them with anxious effort and unnatural strain.

Some wise individuals realize that hard work, all by itself, is no virtue. They are the alert ones. They see the difference between anxious striving and natural coasting.

Anxious effort gives you nothing for something.

Natural effort, effort harmonized with the natural laws of life, gives you something for nothing.

One task of Psycho-Pictography is to show you that the easy way is the right way. It does not appeal to an unrealistic desire to get something for nothing. It tries to show every man that he inwardly possesses everything he needs, *but does not consciously know it.*

You need not strive to create contentment or energy or friendships or anything else. You need only to claim them. You need not struggle. You need only *realize*. Your lamp is already lighted, and you need only to remove its covering.

Writes philosopher Meher Baba:

> *It must be impressed constantly upon humanity that the real birthright of every man and woman is to achieve his own original freedom, that it can be achieved, and that sooner or later it must be achieved. Without this, there is no lasting escape from the day-to-day problems . . .*[1]

Suppose you knew that a map to a fabulous treasure had been taken to a mountain peak, torn and scattered to the four winds. You would, of course, search for the pieces—but would you strain anxiously at every step, or would you enjoy the adventure? Would you be gloomy, or would you step cheerfully around? Knowing that the treasure *can* be found, you would be excited, but at the same time relaxed. [MENTAL PICTURE 7]

Your treasures of contentment and energy and everything else are yours to find. That is what this chapter—in fact, the entire book—is all about.

Making Your Mind Your Best Friend

Throughout these pages, we will be meeting terms such as *awareness, understanding, perception of Truth, higher levels of consciousness,* and other similar terms. It is important to define them. For maximum clarity, I will phrase the definition in three different ways. Simply remember that they all mean the same thing.

Awareness or understanding or perception of Truth means:
To see something new; something we have never inwardly grasped up to now.
Or:
To so understand an idea that it is no longer intellectual knowledge, but an internally operating fact.
Or:
To actually see a false attitude or viewpoint as false, and a truthful viewpoint as truthful.

---

[1] Meher Baba, *Listen, Humanity,* narrated and edited by D. H. Stevens (New York: Dodd, Mead and Company, 1957).

When we were children, we had certain attitudes toward life; for example, that our parents should buy us every toy in the store window. As our understanding developed, that unrealistic attitude was replaced by genuine understanding. We were, therefore, free from a frustrating demand for toys. That is a simple example of the difference between a mere *attitude* and a mature *understanding*.

Let's take another misunderstanding, common to many people, relating to the mind. People do not realize that the mind can actually be transformed into something entirely different from a mechanically reacting machine. What may now be a man's worst enemy can be amazingly changed into a man's best friend. The very mind that may now be confused or angry or frustrated can be turned into something clear, creative, cheery, unafraid.

Misunderstanding is like a loosely built brick wall. Remove a key brick or two and the whole false structure collapses, enabling you to see beyond to a previously unknown empire.

Sometimes a simple statement of truth is enough to crack open a new world of awareness. I once asked a troubled man, "Did it ever occur to you that life might be *good*, and that you simply do not see it?"

He later reported, "That was like switching on a light bulb that had been out for years."

One of the greatest contributions of Psycho-Pictography is a *new understanding*. A positive Mental Picture attacks and destroys illusions and irritating imaginations.

If we are personally to find this wonderful new life, a new understanding is essential. We must discover who we really are, what we can actually do for ourselves, how we can change and brighten what we may now consider hopeless.

The first heroic step toward self-knowledge is the quiet admission that we presently do not know ourselves very well. Self-honesty is self-power. Armed with it, we can dash courageously into the adventure of self-discovery, certain of victory.

Try this for an encouraging truth: *No sincere effort toward self-understanding is ever lost.* It remains as an energizing force. This is such an inspiring idea that I want to repeat it: *Once glimpsed, a new truth can never be lost.* "Knowledge comes, but wisdom lingers." (Alfred Lord Tennyson)

It is like viewing a spacious, beautiful countryside as you pass in your car. Once seen, it can never be unseen. Whether you are consciously aware of it or not, it remains to guide and inspire.

Picture yourself standing in a long, dark hall with dozens of windows covered by drapes. You pull aside one of the drapes to gain a bit of light as well as a first glimpse of the lovely world outside. You uncover a second window to have even more light and land. You pull aside more and more drapes, permitting additional clarity and perception. [MENTAL PICTURE 8]

That illustrates the positive pleasure of awareness, of inner perception. Work to gain more. Understanding is the golden touch that transforms you and your world. Understanding has a very distinct feeling; it is a unique process.

It changes you—internally and outwardly—into the kind of person you want to be.

How to Achieve Natural Happiness

"I would like," said Morton H., "a clear picture of the change from unhappiness to happiness. Can you give us an example of how we reclaim our happy True Self?"

"It is the lightening of inner loads you are now unconsciously carrying around. Most people are not aware of all the useless burdens that wear them down."

"Like negative emotions?"

"And fearful imaginations and frozen attitudes. As you become conscious of these pointless burdens, you drop them. Remember, no man *consciously* or *knowingly* burdens himself. He doesn't see what he is doing to himself."

"I have a glimpse of that," commented Morton. "I once saw the folly of always rushing around, of inventing useless activities just to keep my mind distracted. I saw that I wasn't rushing *toward* anything, but rather *away* from my unhappy self. Now, I've learned to like my own company. But you said that we must lighten these negative loads?"

Yes. Picture it like this: You are flying in an airplane carrying excessive cargo. It wobbles, stalls, dips dangerously toward

THE ONE WAY TO GET SOMETHING FOR NOTHING // 19

earth. You looked into the problem. You see that the danger is not in the natural power of the plane, but in the unwise overloading. So you drop a few crates. The airplane rises, becomes a bit steadier. You drop more crates. The craft responds by rising higher and flying smoother. Finally, you rid it of all unwise cargo. Now, you have a swift and safe flight. [MENTAL PICTURE 9]

That is what we can do for our own natural happiness. We can lighten ourselves. *We must become aware of our totally unnecessary loads of negativity.* As we do, we toss them overboard. No man *knowingly* burdens himself. Then, we soar freely and securely.

The authors of *Zen Buddhism and Psychoanalysis* express the same idea like this:

> To "become conscious of the unconscious" means to overcome repressedness and alienation from myself, and hence from the stranger. It means to wake up, to shed illusions, fictions, and lies, to see reality as it is. The man who wakes up is the liberated man, the man whose freedom cannot be restricted either by others or by himself. The process of becoming aware of that which one was not aware of constitutes the inner revolution of man. It is the true awakening which is at the root of both creative intellectual thought and intuitive immediate grasp.[2]

Recognizing Your True Self vs. Your False Self

It is essential to understand that everyone has both a True Self and a False Self. Nothing is more important to investigate and to understand than this. The stronger the True Self, the happier and more productive the man in every department of life. To the degree that the False Self dominates, to that same extent a man is frustrated, the more he feels life empty and futile.

The True Self is the essential you. It is entirely free of all negative emotions, such as panic and despair. You were born with the True Self. It is the real you. *It can never be lost,* though it may be presently dominated by the False Self.

The False Self is the cause of every trouble you have. You must

[2] D. T. Suzuki, Erich Fromm, and Richard De Martino, *Zen Buddhism and Psychoanalysis* (New York: Harper and Row, Publishers, Incorporated, 1960).

try to see this. When you do see it, you will never again blame yourself or anyone else for anything that happens. Because you are no longer identified with the False Self—that is, because you no longer take it as *you*—you simply see that *it* acted unwisely or angrily or even foolishly. The False Self is merely your *acquired* attitudes and beliefs; *it is not the real you.*

The False Self has been called by many names. The New Testament refers to it as the old nature. A modern psychologist would call it the negatively conditioned self. When we say that someone acts egotistically we are referring to a feature of the False Self. All mental, emotional, and physical action springing from the False Self does damage. All action arising from the True Self enriches you.

Question: "How does all this connect with personal happiness?"

Answer: "The entire process of becoming happy consists in gradually weakening the False Self so that the True Self regains its rightful position in your life. The False Self is always unhappy. The True Self is never anything but happy."

Back in 1904 a scientist named A. V. L. Verneuil invented synthetic rubies. They were so similar to natural rubies that they nearly knocked the bottom out of the market for the natural gems. Nobody could tell the difference. The world of commercial rubies was thrown into panic and confusion.

Finally, some gem experts took their instruments and went to work on the synthetic stones. They made an interesting discovery. Deep down inside the man-made gems were some defects consisting of tiny bubbles. They broadcast their discovery. Instantly, the price of natural rubies soared to its original high mark. Now that it was possible to tell the difference between the artificial and the real, no one wanted the false gems. Everyone desired the real, the natural, the genuinely valuable rubies. [MENTAL PICTURE 10]

That is how we can go at it. We can take courage to look deeply inside ourselves. Then we will see the difference between our real and our artificial personalities. Once we see it—*once we really see it*—we no longer value false ideas or attitudes. We want only the valuable emotions, the enriching thoughts, the beneficial interests and peaceful desires.

Remember, it is *awareness of the difference between the two* that gets us on the right track.

You now possess both the intelligence and the inclination to liberate yourself from the bondage of the False Self. Even if you have doubts, you need not fear them; even if you feel helpless, you need not hesitate; even if you don't know what to do, you need not despair.

Your True Self always knows just what to do, even when you don't. Why not listen when it speaks?

Why It's True That You Lack Nothing!

"You lack nothing. Everything you need for a rich and abundant life is already supplied. You have them *now*."

These ideas given by me at a lecture produced the following question from a man with a puzzled frown: "But if we have everything we need, why don't we *experience* them in a practical way? Take our energies. Why do I tire so easily? Not only physically, but mentally and emotionally. It's not just me; almost everyone complains of weariness. You say that we lack nothing. I don't understand. Will you please explain?"

"The only valid tiredness is that normal, physical weariness you have after working hard. All else is totally unnecessary. When you experience normal physical tiredness, bedtime is welcome. But not so with emotional fatigue. Facing bedtime is a nightly nightmare with millions of emotionally worn-out people. That's because they know they face another sleepless night."

"But what about all this rich energy? How can we experience it in our daily affairs?"

"First, by being aware of how you yourself waste your natural supply. Then, by knowing how to stop it."

"How do we waste ourselves?"

"With negative emotions. You get up in the morning with a fresh supply of strength. Then, you get upset over a spilled cup of coffee. Already you have lost vital power. Later, you angrily reflect on how badly someone treated you. More loss. That evening you worry over a domestic problem. And so it goes. One negative feeling after another, each draining away your strength and good humor. No wonder you're tired!"

"How can we stop exhausting ourselves?"

How To Stop Tiring Yourself Needlessly

"By thinking in a new way toward everything that happens. And I mean *everything*. Remember, regardless of what happens, you need not respond with life-robbing emotions. A principal aim of our meetings is to retrain the mind so that it *thinks in a new way*. When this happens, natural energies are retained for constructive purposes."

Strength and energy are but two examples of something for nothing. You have no lack of energy whatsoever. You can experiment heroically with this truth by refusing to go along with the temptation to become negative. Try it. Just try it. You will delightfully discover that you really have the strength to refuse to lose your strength!

Speaking of a man with such wise heroism, author Colin Wilson writes:

> He comes to recognize the energy-stealing emotions, all the emotions that do not make for inwardness, and he sets out to exterminate them in himself. As he moves toward his objective, he increases steadily his supply of surplus vital power, and so increases his powers of foresight and hindsight . . . there is a breaking-free of the body's sense of imprisonment in time and raising warmth of life-energy that is spoken of in the Gospel as "to have life more abundantly." [8]

You Are a Mental Millionaire

At this point, I want to give you one of the most amazing of all Mental Pictures. This section should receive extra attention as you review this book. Give its ideas time to work. You will then discover that you are really a mental millionaire.

Picture a man standing outside a bank. In his conversations with other people he remarks that he has a million dollars on deposit in the bank. But he really doesn't believe it; he is merely trying to convince himself and others that he is a millionaire.

[8] Colin Wilson, *The Outsider* (Boston: Houghton Mifflin Company, 1956).

Next, picture that man stepping inside the bank to transact some small business. To his surprise and joy he is told that he actually has a million dollars in his account. It is an inheritance that he had carelessly ignored for many years.

He discovers that he really is the very millionaire he pretended to be! [MENTAL PICTURE 11]

That is man's strange position in the world. He pretends that he is happy or wise or peaceful, but secretly feels that it is all a fake. But here is one of the most delightfully startling thoughts you will ever meet: *Every man really is a mental millionaire; he really does possess happiness and wisdom and peace.* But he never knows it as a personal experience because he indulges in the utterly fantastic act of *pretending to be something that he really is!*

This makes clear the need for dropping all pretenses in order to find the True Self. People are afraid to stop pretending because they fear that behind it lies only emptiness. But behind it lies richness, the real kind. The situation can also be compared with a beautiful woman who wears a beautiful mask because she doesn't realize that she herself is really beautiful. If she took courage enough to drop the mask, she would find her lovely True Self. Every woman is beautiful, if she only knew it. Every man is a mental millionaire, if only he would stop pretending and start claiming.

The Point of It All

Asked someone, "Why do we fail to make this claim?"

"Because you think that pretense is all you have, all that exists. You mistakenly assume that you would be impoverished without it. But you can change; you can think and see differently. Get emotionally aggressive against these pretenses that cheat you of the real thing. Rebel against your own stage-acting. Claim your True Self *now*. Then you will see that you really are a mental millionaire—and were one all along."

I want to break into the text of this book to talk personally for a moment with you, the reader.

Perhaps, as you have read along, a certain question has arisen in your mind. Many people ask this particular question in letters and at meetings. I'd like to discuss it with you. It goes like this:

Mr. Howard, I am sometimes confused about my purpose in studying these ideas. Why am I working at self-understanding, at changing my attitudes, at dropping false beliefs? What is the value? Why should I work? Why persist? In other words, *what is the point of it all?*

The point is very simple. In fact, it is so simple that many people miss it.

The point is to *live the way you really want to live.*

> You want a brighter tomorrow.
> That is the point.
> You want control of your own life.
> That is the point.
> You want to avoid mistakes.
> To live with simplicity.
> To have abundant energy.
> To be youthful.
> To be free of pressure.
> To know who you are.
> To be unafraid.

That is the point of it all.
And you can have it all.

Don't complicate things by thinking that there is any other point. There isn't. Be practical. See clearly and directly that the entire point is to have what you really want. As you read this book, stick to this single point. Then, you will have what you really want.

The Power of Doing Nothing

"I hope this doesn't sound like a silly question," said Norman E., "but what should I do about a problem when I haven't the sligntest idea of what to do?"

"Why do anything at all?"

"Well, don't we have to take action? The problem won't solve itself, will it?"

"It will, once you know the secret. Sometimes the correct action is no action at all. Inaction can be a creative process. It can lead to a surprising solution, for instance, instead of supplying an answer, it dissolves the very problem. You see, we are so anxious to *do* something about a problem. We don't like the tension and the suspense. We will do almost anything to settle the matter one way or another. But this leads to poor judgments and impulsive actions that only deepen the difficulty."

"Yes, I've seen that happen more than once."

"Work at *not* doing the things you usually do. If your habitual actions fail to clear the air, why continue with them? Strike out in an entirely new direction; that is, don't do the usual things that lead to the usually unhappy results. Give your mind a chance to clear itself; don't be so eager to get a result. The answer is already within you, but you won't see it as long as you chase frantically around looking for it. It's like trying to recover a coin resting at the bottom of a pool. If you anxiously splash around, you cannot see it. But if you wait, if you remain alertly inactive, if you cease to stir the water, the coin will become visible. Then, the very seeing of it is the same thing as its recovery."

"Could we call it the power of doing nothing?"

"Yes. See the process as constructive inaction."

"Can you give a practical example of all this?"

"Suppose a man has domestic problems. There are family quarrels that keep everyone unhappy. He becomes aware that his usual actions—perhaps attempts to dominate others—are useless. They only increase the difficulty. So he wisely stops using this wrong method. He drops it as inadequate. Now, the quietness produced by this *not doing* will give him clearer insight. He might see, for the first time, that it is far more important to have a happy home than to be a domestic dictator."

All this is a major secret of this book: We must replace habitual action with fresh insight. By not doing the usual, we discover the unusual that clears our difficulties.

"Do not strive to seek the true," wrote a Zen teacher, "only cease to cherish opinions." This confirms a point covered in other pages: *freedom is a shedding process.* We need only set aside the false opinions we have about ourselves and about the world in which we live. Then, having made room for Truth, it comes.

How To Be A Hero

Have you ever noticed the similarity between a detective novel and the mystery of life? The idea makes an interesting excursion.

A detective story begins relatively peacefully. The stage is set, and the hero or heroine is brought onstage. You then meet various characters who revolve around the hero in major or minor roles. There are good and bad people; you meet characters whom you like and others whom you suspect of being other than they pretend to be.

Trouble arrives. Someone gets a poison-pen letter. A young woman is attacked on a lonely road. Strange sounds drift down from the attic. A fleeting figure is barely seen as it darts behind a statue in the dark garden. Someone screams.

And somewhere, in the dim shadows, lurks the criminal behind it all. Sly and skillful, he possesses a high but evil intellect. When attacking the hero, his method is stealth, and his purpose is destruction. He operates by boldness and bluff.

For a while, the hero is confused—but not disheartened. Because he gets tired of taking it, because he resolves to no longer live in fear, he goes into action. He rebels against his own complacency—and directs all that rebellious energy against the lurking criminal.

At first, the clues are meager. But he persists. He tracks down clues, studies human nature, forces himself to strike out in new directions. The clues pay off. He recognizes a familiar voice and locates a hidden room.

Finally, the hero wins. The criminal is exposed. The novel ends happily. [MENTAL PICTURE 12]

In life, the hero is the True Self. The False Self is the destructive criminal. In the novel, the hero always wins. In life, the True Self can always win—if it persists. A man wanting to solve his inner mysteries need only start with what few clues he has, or none at all. At the start of a mystery novel, you never ask the outcome; likewise, in life you need never wonder whether there exists a happy solution to your problems. It is there, if you only know it—if only you will plunge heroically after the clues!

How To Dissolve Disappointments

The purpose of Psycho-Pictography is to empower you to think on a newer and higher level, to change your values and viewpoints, to cast aside unworkable ideas and to think from practical ones. This, whether one presently realizes it or not, is what really changes everything wonderfully. So let's take a very common problem of life and see how Larry G. changed his life by changing his thoughts.

"What," he asked, "about the little daily disappointments that we all have? Can they be abolished? I have no overwhelming problems; just a series of little nagging ones. You know what I mean—someone makes a promise and then breaks his word. I don't understand how a fresh viewpoint can cancel out disappointments, but I want to find out."

"All right. Please follow. The fact is, someone breaks his promise to you. I assure you that it is not the bare fact of that broken promise that hurts. The disappointment comes when your mind *adds* something to that fact. The fact has no power to hurt you; it's your mental *addition* that does the damage."

"Please explain."

"He breaks his promise to you. That is the bare fact. It cannot hurt you in any way whatsoever. But your mind quickly *adds something* to that fact. For instance, you might think that he doesn't value you enough to keep his word. Or you might suspect that he's trying to cheat you out of something. Again, you might indignantly think that here is just another instance of how unfair the world is to you."

Larry, who had attended meetings, smiled and asked, "Is that the pride and vanity of the False Self?"

"That is a very good observation. Your insight is growing. Yes, the False Self demands a certain behavior from others. When others don't agree, it becomes disappointed, even enraged. Of course, the person living in the False Self hasn't the faintest idea of how he harms himself."

Larry faithfully worked with the idea: *see the bare fact, but don't add to it.* He found, of course, great changes, and reported, "There are no longer any disappointments, only events."

You, too, can dissolve disappointments by not mentally adding to your daily events.

Just as all the colors necessary for a beautiful painting are present in the artist's palette, so do you now possess everything needed for a wonderful life. You can become the skilled artist who paints a new life-picture for himself. Such artistic ability is natural to you.

HELPFUL POINTS TO REMEMBER

1. The easy way is the right way.
2. Understanding is one of the greatest forces on earth. Build your understanding.
3. You can change into the kind of person you want to be. Let Psycho-Pictography aid you.
4. Review the enormously beneficial ideas about the True Self and the False Self.
5. Your True Self knows all the answers you need.
6. Recognize your richness of natural energy. Get rid of strength-robbing negativities.
7. You are now a mental millionaire.
8. The point of your life is to live the way you really want to live.
9. Discover the marvelous technique of doing nothing. It is a surprising power for success.
10. Dissolve disappointments with the technique supplied in this chapter.

3

How to Face and Overcome Life's Crises

A man doesn't live his particular kind of life because he likes it.

He lives as he does because he thinks there is nothing better.

Pause and consider this idea. A tremendous clue to lofty living is hidden within.

The purpose of Psycho-Pictography is to show you how to make a grand reversal.

Instead of thinking there is nothing better, you will actually live in that superior state.

Making Accurate Decisions

Let's start with the inquiry, "Will you please clarify the state of the unhappy person? I mean, tell us about the inner conditions that keep us running from one painful crisis to the next."

"The inner state of a troubled person can be described in many ways, but they all mean the same thing. Here are a few: He possesses inner contradictions that he can neither endure nor escape. He has lost touch with his True Self. He fails to see that the torture *of* himself is *by* himself. He wanders from one false trail to another. He walks in nightmarish sleep."

A woman in my audience smiled. "That describes me exactly," she said. "Can you also summarize the way out of this nightmare? Could we have some short and meaningful points?"

"Honestly face your inner contradictions; don't pretend they don't exist. Have the courage to strike out in the new direction whispered by your True Self. Dare to take your own life into your own hands. Stop conforming. Don't let inner pressures goad you into unwise decisions. Dare to abandon your rigid ways of thinking. Walk forward with the simple truth that the good life awaits you."

Let's take one of the above ideas for special study. It has secret power for preventing a personal crisis: *Don't let inner pressures goad you into unwise decisions.*

Let's suppose that you come to a fork in your mental road where you must make a decision.

You must never decide in a way that merely lifts the pressure of indecision.

This is the unfortunate choice that many people make. They are interested only in *immediate relief,* not *final accuracy.* But you must not do this. A decision based on relief alone is almost always against your best interests. It not only fails to settle the immediate crisis but tends to create more problems. It pyramids the original crisis. It also causes regret, as reported by one woman, "I used to buy my clothes impulsively, just to get them out of my mind. The minute I got home I regretted my choice. Now, I'm wiser. If I don't really know what I want, I buy nothing."

Be aware that indecision is a pressure. Don't make a decision merely to relieve that pressure. Be wise. Wait. Be calm. Think. Don't rush impulsively to get it done. Don't race for the nearest answer. Let the right answer come to you. It will.

How to Know All the Answers

Someone asked, "Please give us an example of unclear thinking toward a course of action."

"Thinking that a new course of action is *better,* when it is only *different.* That's like deciding that it is better to jump into a swamp than into a bog. The wise man jumps into neither."

Your inner self, your True Self, knows all the answers. It never makes a mistake. This is an absolute fact, whether you realize it or not. It is good to realize it. Find this all-wise True Self and you will never again face a decision-crisis. Not only that, but what pleasure you have in your own company!

Here is how Dr. Erich Fromm explains the process:

> *Only those qualities that result from our spontaneous activity give strength to the self and thereby form the basis of its integrity. The inability to act spontaneously, to express what one genuinely feels and thinks, and the resulting necessity to present a pseudo self to others and oneself, are the root of the feeling of inferiority and weakness. Whether or not we are aware of it, there is nothing of which we are more ashamed than of not being ourselves, and there is nothing that gives us greater pride and happiness than to think, to feel, and to say what is ours.*[1]

Don't be your usual, habitual, repetitious thoughts. Be *yourself.* There is, you know, a great difference in the two.

As you know, an earthquake occurs whenever a fault in the earth shifts suddenly. The sliding of an unsettled section beneath the surface jolts everything above. An earthquake is caused by a false foundation.

That is similar to what happens when a human being gets jolted by a personal crisis. The subconscious areas of the mind rest on a faulty foundation, so any sudden crisis causes upheaval. It jolts the man into damaging behavior, including nervousness and distress.

Happily, there is a major difference between a physical earthquake and a psychological one. The human earthquake has a sure cure. The fault can be removed. A man need not live in fear of periodic disturbance. He can be settled upon the foundation of psychological reality. [MENTAL PICTURE 13]

I want to give you a superb example of this. It relates to the question of personal morality. No other crisis causes so much painful anxiety and useless guilt.

---

[1] Erich Fromm, *Escape From Freedom* (New York: Holt, Rinehart and Winston, Inc., 1941).

The question came up, "I'm confused about morality. What, exactly, is right and what is wrong? I have a strong urge to break away from my habitual life. What about this urge? Is it immoral?"

"Why don't you go ahead and break away? Why not live the way you really want to?"

"I'd like to, but . . ."

"Would you like to hear why you don't?"

Several people called, "Yes!"

"You have a false sense of morality. Society has imposed upon you its hypocritical standards of conduct, which you fearfully take as true. This makes you feel guilty, anxious, afraid. Society sets up an ideal, like a tall stone statue, then tells you to look like that. But you can't maintain your inner integrity and look like that. The statue is idealistic nonsense. Then, when you fail to hold that statue-like pose, you feel guilty and resentful. All statues are evasions of genuine morality. They are illusions. No one can live up to an illusion."

Don't Fall for Demands To Be Unselfish

"Another hypocritical morality is when other people press upon you a false sense of duty. They tell you what you owe them. *Think! They* tell *you* what *you* owe *them.* Don't fall for it. The simple truth is, they want something from you, though they call it by a noble name. You owe them nothing. Your first duty is toward yourself, your inner freedom. That is the same as saying that your first duty is toward the Truth."

A woman asked, "This is off the point somewhat, but what attitude should we have toward people who planted those false ideas in our mind, who used us for their own selfish purposes?"

"Simply see that they are asleep. Someone misinformed them, just as they misinformed you. So there is no one to blame. But once *you* see that you were fed false ideas, it is your heroic responsibility to smash the painful pattern. Don't pass it on to your children—if you really love them."

"Then what is genuine morality? How should we behave?"

"Never do anything that harms either yourself or another person. This idea is deeper than you think. Unawakened people don't realize the harm that goes on. A man must wake up. Then, he is happy at last."

How to Make Your Life Trouble-Free

Raise your level of thinking. Uplift your viewpoints. Climb the ladder of self-understanding. Ascend to a higher state of awareness. Glimpse the loftier world.

That is what we have been covering together, time and time again, throughout these pages.

Why? Why all this emphasis on lifting *yourself*, rather than working on surrounding circumstances? *Because you make your circumstances whatever they are.* You live in both a material and a psychological world of your own creation. This means that you can create a new world for yourself that is free from crisis and difficulty! You can move up to a trouble-free level. You really can.

We have a perfect illustration:

The citizens of a village in a deep valley were troubled. Floods regularly swept down the valley to carry away their homes and livestock. Great boulders from the mountain slopes thudded into their streets and yards. Their children stumbled into the marshes.

It was a hard life, but the only one they knew. But one day a Man with Insight came to town. He told them, "The problem is not the floods and boulders and marshes. The problem is you. You are unnecessarily living on a low level."

"An unnecessary low level?" they echoed.

"Yes. Try to understand. Your low level involves you in one crisis after another. As long as you dwell down here, you will have trouble. Raise *yourself*. Problems will cease to happen."

"Show us how!" they pleaded.

So the Man with Insight showed them how to build homes above the valley and on the mountain slopes. Some built new homes a short way above the level of the valley. Others, more wise, built new homes far up the mountainside.

"Now," said the Man with Insight, "you will experience the trouble-free life. By moving your residence, you have removed the problems."

"Yes," someone remarked, "how clear it now is."

"I wonder," someone else added, "why we didn't see it before?" [MENTAL PICTURE 14]

Remember that story. It points the way to freedom from difficulties of every kind. There is no crisis in your life that a higher level of thinking cannot cure. Prove it for yourself.

How to Know What You Want

"What," I asked the meeting one night, "is your single greatest problem?" The answers came:

"To avoid making mistakes."
"I think I feel too much guilt."
"To find more leisure time."
"I don't know what I want from life."
"To earn more money."
"I want people to leave me alone."
"My greatest problem is women."

The last one, spoken by a real estate agent, made everyone laugh. But, by mutual consent, we chose to discuss the fourth problem: "I don't know what I want from life."

"How can you know what you want? Happily, the problem solves itself as you continue with Psycho-Pictography. How come? Because all your wants and desires and wishes and ambitions are based on the way you *think*. But as you learn to think differently, from a high level of understanding, *your desires change*. They become more mature and realistic, but this does not mean that they give you less satisfaction, rather, they are far more pleasurable. Why? Because they now serve your *best* interests, not your ego-centered interests."

"I see that perfectly," commented a woman down front. "I used to agonize over my ambition to be a famous singer. That served my ego-interest but not my best-interest. Now I'm content to sing whenever invited, but I'm no longer offended whenever I'm not asked."

Imagine yourself surrounded by a crowd of people. A dozen voices shout at once, telling you what you want. They insist that you want fame, fortune, power, and so on. You spin around, believing each voice in turn. No wonder you're bewildered. But you get tired of all the shouting, so you slowly walk away. The voices become fainter and fainter. Finally—for the first time in your life—you hear *yourself*. And now—

great day—this inner voice tells you what you really want from life. Now, let me ask you a question: Now that you can hear your inner voice, what does it tell you that you want? [MENTAL PICTURE 15]

How Not Thinking Helps

Next, I want to give you a startling technique for handling any kind of crisis. It may be entirely new to you. Its value cannot be overestimated. The next time you run into a crisis:

Don't be afraid *not* to think about it.
Don't let your thoughts chase around in circles in a frantic attempt to catch an answer.

This is an extremely profound idea, so let's explore it together carefully.

A problem existing on the level of conditioned thinking cannot be solved by conditioned thinking. *A problem cannot be solved on its own level.* It cannot be done any more than a man can lift himself by pulling upward on his legs. Something higher, something outside himself, must be contacted.

That something is *awareness.*

Awareness does far more than supply a temporary answer to a crisis. It dissolves it once and for all. A business acquaintance of mine was worried whether or not he should buy a certain piece of property. He became aware of his *real* motive for wanting it: It would please his vanity. Since that wasn't a practical reason, he didn't buy. His self-awareness solved his problem and possibly saved him from financial loss.

Here is what we must do: we must get our usual, conditioned, limited thoughts out of the way. We must become mentally silent. That silence leaves room for the voice of wisdom from within. Nothing is more practical in everyday affairs than this inner voice.

By refusing to chase around mentally, you gradually weaken the power of useless thoughts. False ideas can be compared with a huge fan whirling at furious speed. It blows out a destructive gale. But if you don't empower that wheel, it slows down, loses its destructive force.

So don't be afraid to *not* think about a difficulty. It is really strange the fear people have of *not* thinking; they are hypnotized by a problem. People get anxious when urged to abandon their habitual thought processes. They assume there is nothing better. But there is. There is awareness. (See Chapter 10 for more details on the difference between thought and awareness.)

This kind of *not thinking* is not an evasion of the difficulty, but a receptivity to a new way of seeing it.

You can, if you like, consider awareness as a *higher form of thinking*. What superiority! It is like an invisible rope overhead. You can reach up and swing over every crisis. Instead of colliding with daily events, you swing easily over them.

Nothing Need Bother You

A magazine article tells about Baron Manfred von Richthofen, the German air act of World War 1. As commander of the famous Flying Circus, he instructed his pilots, "Keep your head and eyes moving around. Be awake to everything. You must never be caught unaware. This does not mean you should be *afraid*. It means you should be *alert*. That is how to have a safe flight." [MENTAL PICTURE 16]

That is a good parallel to how *we* must fly. We need not be anxious about anything, but we must be alert to everything. Alert to what? To opportunities for clearing our lives of everything bothersome. If we take these daily opportunities, we can uplift ourselves before our very eyes.

For instance, alertness toward our *reactions* is of rich profit. Let's see how it cleared the air for Ralph E.

Ralph occupied a desk in a large insurance office. He described his situation, "I'd give anything to break the string of disturbances down at the office. You know what I mean. Someone demands a certain report right now. Someone else drops by to ask why I handled a matter the way I did. To top it all, the company restaurant is out of my favorite dessert!" Ralph laughed. "I'm not feeling sorry for myself. I just wonder why I have to put up with one bother after another?"

"You really don't."

"How come? I can't change these outer events."

"You can stop reacting to them the way you do. You may not

grasp it as yet, but the events themselves don't bother you; it's your own way of reacting. Try to be aware of how you take things. See that the bother is in *you*, not in the incident. This is a major secret for establishing permanent peace of mind. Work with one little annoyance at a time. Try *not* to react with your usual annoyance."

How to Use Mental Magic

When you understand your mind, you understand everything.

Suppose you hand binoculars to a small child without explaining their use. He might try to chew them or pound with them on the floor. Now, binoculars are quite capable of visual magic, but only when used properly. If the child doesn't understand their use, he cannot enjoy their visual magic. But when someone explains the correct function of those binoculars, the child places them to his eyes. He then enjoys a wonderful new world, superbly unlike anything he had ever seen before. [MENTAL PICTURE 17]

It is that way with the human mind. There is nothing wrong with human affairs that mental understanding cannot correct. But people don't believe this. They don't see it. They think that they must change the exterior world. They never suspect that they must use their minds properly; they must start seeing the world in a different way.

As we see the world with this magical mental vision, it changes before our eyes. This change is very practical and delightful. Every area of external living takes on a bright, new look. Because *you* are different, everything else is different. As examples, you will:

1. Make accurate decisions
2. Be alert to opportunities
3. Handle people skillfully
4. Not waste emotional energy
5. Make maximum use of time
6. Think clearly and accurately
7. Have natural enthusiasm
8. Enjoy business enterprises

9. Never be gloomy
10. Build over-all efficiency

Every man is a mental magician. By the dramatic act of changing his mind, he changes his exterior world. It is not necessary that you believe this to be true, but it is necessary that you practice the act. Then you will see what a mental magician you actually are.

How Harry Conquered Depression

One evening after a meeting we were seated around with refreshments. Someone asked Harry C., a successful businessman, "With all your busy financial affairs, how come you never miss a meeting?"

He gestured and said, "I can't afford to miss. I haven't the slightest intention of going back to that stupid depression I used to know." He added, "It's no great problem for people to earn enough money for a comfortable living, but what a problem to *enjoy* their money-making activities! What's the sense of knocking yourself out for eight hours a day just for a short evening of relaxation? Why not enjoy yourself all day long?"

Everyone in the room was impressed by that bit of wisdom. It reminded me of a question Harry had asked during another meeting.

"Why do you speak so often about negative emotions?"

"Because there is a way out of every negative habit of emotion. That is why we are here—to find the way out."

"What about depression? What is the way out?"

"Whenever you feel depressed, don't identify with the state. Let me explain. Whenever depression floods in, don't automatically assume that *you* are the depression. Do not say, '*I* am depressed.' This harmfully identifies you with the state; that is, you and the state are so close together that you can't observe it in yourself. Instead, separate *yourself* from the *feeling of depression*. See it as something entirely apart from yourself; see it as a wind passing through you, but not stopping. That breaks the identification, and it breaks the totally needless habit of depression. Only the False Self is depressed, never the True Self."

You, the reader, can experiment with this for yourself. Don't think that you and your depression are the same thing. You are not your depression any more than you are the wind you feel on a wintry day.

Overcoming Feelings of Helplessness

One of the most painful emotions a human being can experience is that of helplessness. As a further complication, helplessness creates pressure that explodes outwardly with other negative emotions such as hostility and accusation. So, by solving the problem of helplessness, we automatically erase other negativities that spring from it.

The counterattack to helplessness is a glimpse of your True Self, which is all-powerful. Your True Self is the very Truth itself. Paracelsus, the wise Swiss philosopher, points out, "Each man has all the wisdom of the world in himself." Even the slightest perception of higher powers within will energize a man with fresh courage.

A lumber company down in Guatemala had set up a jungle camp for the purpose of cutting rare wood. They were far away from civilization, consequently, it was an expensive project that had to proceed efficiently. But suddenly, while cutting timber, the saws stopped. Workmen stood around helplessly. A frantic message was dispatched to their power plant, some distance away: "Send power." The reply came back: "Check connection." They investigated the cable and found the source of their helplessness—a loose connection. [MENTAL PICTURE 18]

You thrill a man when you tell him that he really has all the power he needs for a victorious life. A statement like that arouses the True Self that knows it to be an absolute fact. But a man must persist beyond this first thrill. He cannot coast upon it. He must continue to nourish the source of that genuine thrill; he must enthusiastically want to know more of it. It would do those jungle workers no good merely to thrill at glimpsing the power plant in the distance. A firm and permanent connection was necessary. Likewise, when you make a firm connection with the only source of genuine power—your True Self—feelings of helplessness vanish forever.

Always take the viewpoint that any good idea may have deeper significance than it first appears to have. The idea of a firm connection with your True Self is a good place to start.

Are You Taking These Ideas Home?

Imagine yourself shopping in a large, modern market. First you place a few staple items in your shopping cart, like milk and bread. The idea of fresh fruit appeals, so you add some apples and peaches. Because you like your foods spicy, some cinnamon and ginger pop into the cart. Finally, you think you'd like something sweet, so you add a chocolate cake.

Your shopping cart is now loaded with good things. You wheel it to the checker, pay your money, and prepare to take it home.

At this point, suppose you do an incredible thing. Suppose you simply walk out of the market without taking your groceries. Suppose you don't take them home? You wouldn't dream of such an act, of course. After spending both your time and money, you would think it fantastic not to bring home the groceries. You would carry them home to be enjoyed. [MENTAL PICTURE 19]

As you cover the principles of these pages, let that picture impress you. These principles and truths and techniques are for your health and enjoyment. You need them. Not only that, but you have paid for them with your careful examination.

Do not leave these ideas in the book. Take them home; that is, apply them in your everyday experience. *That* is where they nourish you. Just as groceries must be taken home, so must these ideas be taken into your mental home.

Take the dynamic truth that no one can hurt or insult you unless you unknowingly grant them the power of insult. Suppose you have taken this idea home. In this case, you realize that only the False Self, with its touchy vanity, gets insulted. Your insight causes that useless self to disappear. So, insults and criticisms vanish into thin air!

What a fantastically free life awaits the man or woman who carries home this truth, or any other!

Have you done so?

Well, why not? Don't leave it in the print of these pages. It is yours. You have paid. Take it home to enjoy!

SUMMARY OF VITAL TRUTHS

1. Do not permit a crisis to goad you into impulsive actions. Think calmly and wisely.
2. You have a right to live your own life, as long as it harms neither yourself nor others.
3. Your first duty is toward your own inner development.
4. It is entirely possible for you to live unburdened by one crisis after another.
5. Use the startling technique of not thinking. Replace habitual thought by new awareness.
6. Remember how Ralph E. cleared a crisis from his daily affairs.
7. Review the list of ten benefits arising from your uplifted vision.
8. Try to see depression as a passing feeling. Do not see it as a permanent part of yourself.
9. Your True Self can meet and dissolve every crisis.
10. Take all these ideas into your mental home. They become your willing servants.

4

How to Break
Self-Defeating Habits

The story is told of a man who lived in a home having mirrors as walls. Whatever room he entered, he saw himself reflected in a mirror. He spent his time looking at himself from this angle and from that viewpoint. Day and night he saw only himself.

At first it was a highly gratifying experience. His own image was the only thing in the world. Nothing existed outside himself. He was the sole object of attention and admiration.

But after a while, a strange anxiety set in. The thrill of seeing only himself turned into a dull habit, then into desperate pain. What had once been a thrilling gratification had now become a terror. Loneliness entered. He felt depressed, but worst of all, he felt trapped.

One day a furious rebellion swept through him. Taking stones, he hurled them against the mirrors, revealing an entirely new world on the outside. Having broken his habitual self-imprisonment, he enjoyed his new world. [MENTAL PICTURE 20]

This chapter reveals an entirely new method for breaking habitual living patterns. In keeping with a basic principle of Psycho-Pictography, our purpose is to change ourselves. People often ask, "Why am I such a slave to my habits?" and "Is there a way out of this daily grind that really gets me nowhere?"

I assure you that there is a way out.

Simply defined, a habit is a repeated way of doing something—of thinking, acting, feeling, responding, and so on. There are beneficial habits, such as finding right procedures and abandoning wrong ones. There are harmful habits, such as worrying about tomorrow and meeting daily challenges with negative reactions.

How to Conquer Unwanted Habits

Here is great news: All harmful habits *can* be broken. There are no exceptions to this principle. You can, if you want, empty your life of destructive habits, just as you might empty a pail of unwanted junk.

Habits are a result of our conditioning; that is, they were acquired through association with others with the same habits. Habits are usually picked up by imitating other people or by following their example.

There are two ways to conquer unwanted habits. One method is to attack the habitual desire with a new desire. Suppose that you want to stop smoking. You must introduce a new desire that is contrary to the desire to smoke. You could encourage the desire to save money or to show your friends how strong you are, or you might want to improve your health. If any of these are strong enough, you will conquer the habit, for the stronger always overcomes the weaker.

But the far more effective way is through the powerful idea of *non-identification*. This means that you break the habit by ceasing to identify with it. To identify with a habit means that you take the habit as *yourself*—but you are *not* the same thing as your habit. If you have the habit of wearing a green jacket, you are not the same thing as that jacket; you are merely wearing it for a time. Likewise, you are not the same thing as your habit. You and your habit are two entirely separate things. Try to see this.

How to Achieve Non-Identification

Let's continue with this method of non-identification: Do not say, "*I* have a bad temper," or, "*I* am absent-minded." Every time you do this you strengthen the illusion that you and your habit are one and the same thing. But just as you are not that green jacket you are wearing, you are not a habit that you wear on the inner self. Refer to a habit as "it." When speaking of absent-mindedness, say, "It is a present part of my life." This wears down the identification, it separates *you* from the *habit;* you begin to see them as entirely different things. Once your mind glimpses the truth that a habit is merely something acquired, it also sees that it need not be a permanent part of the inner make-up. Since a habit is acquired, it can also be dropped.

A harmful habit, whatever it may be, is part of the False Self. As the False Self is dissolved through Psycho-Pictography, unwanted habits fall away of themselves. So, work on uncovering the True Self. It is entirely free of unwanted habits.

Back in the days of sailing vessels, British and American sea captains were faced with a peculiar problem. In crossing westward from England to Boston, the voyage was much slower than when crossing eastward from Boston to England. In fact, the westward crossing took an additional two weeks, which represented considerable loss of time and energy. The owners of the vessels carried their problem to Benjamin Franklin, who was Deputy Postmaster General at that time. Franklin, in turn, consulted a veteran sea captain named Timothy Folger.

"It takes two weeks longer," explained Folger, "because you don't understand the Gulf Stream. When crossing westward it flows against a ship, costing as much as three miles an hour. Don't fight the Gulf Stream; get outside of it and into the free sea." [MENTAL PICTURE 21]

We need not fight our unwanted habits. As we will see in later pages, a frontal assault only increases their power. We need only sail in natural waters.

The Power of Mental Pictures in Breaking Habits

At this point I want to review with you a few basic ideas about Psycho-Pictography. There is value in reminding ourselves of the miracle method of Mental Pictures.

The ideas you have absorbed have already begun their good work within. According to your receptivity, they have spread their rays into your mind to enlighten it. Perhaps you have already experienced a change or two; for instance, maybe you react with a shade less anxiety to a daily condition. Or maybe you now understand something that you never quite saw before.

Increase your receptivity. You then become like the needle of a compass. No matter how it is turned or twisted by outer elements, it always swings back to point in the right direction.

Our actions in life are a result of the way we see life. No truth is more important to grasp than this. We act toward life, for benefit or loss, according to the way we habitually see things.

Suppose that you are about to enter a roomful of strangers. As you step into that room, a picture flashes into your mind of how you acted on a *previous* entering. That *past* viewpoint now determines your *present* behavior. If you were nervous and uncertain on the previous occasion, that negative image instructs, "You were nervous before, so you must be nervous again;" and that is exactly what will happen.

But suppose you smash that harmful and habitual mental image? Suppose you change it to one of calm confidence? That new mental picture would then work itself out into new and poised behavior.

The way you think determines the way you act. The way you act determines what happens to you. Think well, and you act well. Act well, and all is well.

New Mental Pictures mean a wonderful new life. They turn our received ideas into personal powers. In his essay *Intellect*, Ralph Waldo Emerson speaks of the transfer of truth: "But to make it available it needs a vehicle or art by which it is conveyed to men. To be communicable it must become picture or sensible object."

How to Attain the Habit of Peace

It is helpful to remember that *negative mental pictures are only imaginations.* If a person takes them as real, he gives them false power to frighten him. This fear may then turn into self-harming behavior. Take a person who maintains an image of himself as being cruel. He will then unconsciously act out that image with cruel behavior, which is always self-destructive. He is like a man who burns down his house because he doesn't like a picture he took of it.

But—and this must never be forgotten—all negative imaginations can be shattered. They can be replaced with positive pictures, with the True Self which resides in peace. As one woman phrased it, "The secret magic of mental pictures makes you as free as you used to be."

We must never be afraid of the new truths prompted by Psycho-Pictography; we must never resist them. I mention this because the human mind tends to be shy of the new and strange. But this is like resisting diamonds because we are familiar only with rocks.

As Dr. Fritz Kunkel points out:

> But this new image appears as the inner enemy only as long as the individuals identify themselves with their Egos. The next moment, they may remember that they always felt a longing for a better and deeper life . . . But they wanted to achieve this by self-control and moral practices. Now another avenue is open towards this goal. It comes from inside themselves, not with moral commands but with creative power. It is really their better Self.[1]

Why No One Is Permanently Lost

Mental Pictures help you to find this True Self described by Dr. Kunkel. They destroy painful illusions, they cancel the contradictions of the False Self. Every area of life takes on a new and refreshing look. Let's take a practical example of a helpful Mental Picture:

---

[1] Fritz Kunkel, *In Search of Maturity* (New York: Charles Scribner's Sons, 1943).

Some years ago a statue of a national hero was erected in a South American village. As hard times came, the village was abandoned. Jungle vines crept up to cover and conceal the statue. Its existence was forgotten for many years. Then, someone remembered. The statue's value was discussed and verified. An exploration party was organized to reclaim it. For weeks the explorers chopped their way through the green maze. Their efforts met with reward. The long-lost statue was located. It was cleared of its entanglements and restored to its former glory. [MENTAL PICTURE 22]

Every man or woman is something like that. No one is permanently lost. No mental jungle can withstand the person determined to find his True Self. As a specific instance, a woman told me that she had been lost in the jungle of daily irritability. After working with Mental Pictures she reported, "You know, I'm amazed to find that I need not be lost in irritability. At the end of the day, I wonder why I no longer get quite so angry and upset."

In order to remember your dreams, you must write them down the moment you awaken in the morning. Otherwise, they slip swiftly from memory. The same with the ideas in Psycho-Pictography. Once you grasp the truth of a Mental Picture, try to impress yourself with it. Write it down on a slip of paper. Mark it in the book. Reflect upon it as you go through your day. That makes it a permanent picture with persistent power.

Attracting High-Level Prosperity

Your level of mental awareness attracts the habitual life you lead.

This towering truth is worth days of examination. It can save years of barren effort.

Here we have a secret principle, usually understood only by those who delve deeply into esoteric doctrine. It is a mysterious feature hidden within many well-known teachings, including Christianity, Zen Buddhism, and in the messages of Socrates and Plato. I want to make it very clear to you, so that you can attract an entirely new circle of fortune.

During a battle of the Middle Ages, a king's life was saved by an archer in the ranks. In gratitude, the king declared to the soldier, "Climb up the mountain trail for a period of six hours. All the land that is viewed from the top-most height shall be yours. The higher you ascend the more you possess."

The archer hiked upward, pausing at intervals to rest. At each halt, the king's officers gazed across the countryside, making note of the most distant landmark. The higher the soldier climbed, the more territory the king's men claimed for him. Finally, the soldier possessed a vast area of land with all its natural wealth. [MENTAL PICTURE 23]

Because that soldier acted upon the king's promise, he became wealthy.

I give you a similar promise.

By uplifting your level of mental awareness, you will be rich. You will attract a wider variety of prosperities than you can imagine.

You receive whatever you perceive. In esoteric teachings, *seeing* something is the same thing as *possessing* that something. *Awareness* of a new height automatically returns the profits of that new height.

Your level of mental awareness attracts the habitual life you lead.

Try to see that there are different levels of awareness, of understanding. Also, see that the higher your level of awareness, the more you attract the genuinely good things of life. Some people think that this makes a nice philosophy, but you must do more than this. You must work with it until you experience its rich rewards. It will help your understanding if you remember that, psychologically, like attracts like.

How to Change Everything for the Better

Someone asked, "What sort of things change as I climb to a higher level of understanding?"

"Everything changes. Absolutely everything. Replace an old bouquet of flowers with a fresh one and you have fresh colors, a new arrangement, new charm in every way."

"Will I be more at peace with myself and with the world?"

"This *must* happen. You presently see the world as *you* are.

Uplift what *you* are and you automatically become more peaceful with your world."

"What about material things, like money?"

"You will think clearly toward all financial matters. You will not spend money foolishly because you will know the difference between wise and foolish spending. Money will have its proper place. Whether you have a little or a lot, you will never have emotional conflict over money. Why? Because you are no longer using it for ego-gratification, but simply for practical purposes. This idea has great significance for you. Think it through."

"What about friendships and social relations?"

"They always change for the better. It is a psychological law that you attract people who inhabit your own level of understanding. When you ascend, you attract people on that same higher level. You will find, as you grow, that you drift away from former friends. This is because you no longer have mutual psychological interests. Your new relationships are much happier. There is much less conflict and quarreling so characteristic of a lower level."

"Can these ideas be proven?"

"That is the whole point. I want you to prove them for yourself by personal experience. That is how you win their riches. Do you know what causes you to value these ideas more than anything else? It is when you actually see yourself changing for the better as a result of them! Once you get a taste of truth, nothing can stop you from searching for more. And there is always more. That's the beauty of inner growth; it's an endlessly enjoyable adventure."

"I think that's the point of the Mental Picture about the climbing soldier. By climbing for himself, he proved for himself."

"Right. All this may seem a bit mysterious to you at present, but work with it. Start climbing as best you can. Use the principles of Psycho-Pictography to uplift your level of understanding. Every new level is a delightful surprise."

Psycho-Pictography Changes Your Past!

Nothing arouses more interest and wonderment than the idea we will now explore.

Psycho-Pictography, the miracle method of Mental Pictures,

changes the bothersome past. By teaching a man to see past events through enlightened eyes, these bothersome events lose their power to harm. No longer can a foolish mistake flood a man with painful feelings of regret. Guilt and anxiety—over the worst of folly—vanish completely. A man no longer feels that he has missed the boat, lost the golden opportunity, or been cheated out of anything.

How does this miracle come about? Let's take the case of Ruth B., who, as a young woman, found herself in trouble with a man. Disgraced and ashamed, she moved to a distant city. None of her new friends knew, of course, but she added, "But *I* know. Is there an escape from this hounding guilt?"

"First, Ruth, may I point out that guilt is a deceitful emotion. It is commonly thought to be a sign of humility and repentance, but it is just the opposite. Guilt is a self-centered emotion concerned with what others will think, with reputation, and so on. Not only that, but guilt prevents you from finding freedom from its cause."

"Yes, I can see that. Guilt gets me nowhere. So what do I do?"

"Your freedom lies in not identifying yourself with your past mistake. Let me explain what is meant by the term *identification*. This means that you presently identify *yourself* and your *mistake* as *one;* you take them as the same thing. You wrongly think that *you* are your *mistake*. But you are not. You are not your mistake. Your False Self made that mistake, but you are not your False Self. You see, mistakes like this spring from the False Self which is governed by illusions, impulsiveness, vanity, and just plain foolishness. But your True Self is free of all this. This may be difficult to grasp at first, but please stick with it. You cannot possibly imagine the miracle it will perform for you."

"Can you suggest an easy start, something I can grasp?"

"Don't identify *yourself* as being foolish. See that past event as a foolish act on the part of the False Self—*which is not really you*. Separate the True Self from the False Self."

How to Beat the Problem of Resistance

Ruth's progress can be likened to one of the rivers of the Andes in South America. Starting on a muddy mountain, its yellow water flows down a long valley. As it steadily rolls away from its source, it is fed on both sides by clear, fresh streams. Gradually, the purifying streams transform the river into a natural state of clarity and beauty.

A man's purifying waters are his thoughts of a higher level. They perform the miracle of clearing his past, of giving him a fresh flow today. [MENTAL PICTURE 24]

At this point, I want to explain something helpful for changing not only your past, but the present and the future as well.

Whenever you decide to rebel against a habitual negativity of any kind, a resistance arises within you. You see, negative habits don't want to give up the harmful power they have had over you for so long. They fear extinction. But you must give them no consideration whatsoever. Your peace and progress are at stake.

By understanding that this new resistance is the usual thing, you will not be puzzled or discouraged when it arises. Armed with this understanding, you can cheerfully persist until you crash through the habit barrier.

People are baffled at the difficulty in breaking a mental habit; for instance, that of getting depressed over a business problem. They are even more puzzled at the enormous resistance to their efforts to break the habit. They may succeed for a short time, then, as one woman recently remarked, "I always end up with the same habit of between-meal snacks. I'm like a soldier who decides to give battle but who runs smack into ten enemy soldiers. So I quit. Why fight a losing battle?"

She is right. It is useless to battle like this. A direct attack on a habit only strengthens it. I advised her, "Do not think that the habitual self has power over its habits. Now, since this is so, how can you dissolve the habit?"

"By getting an entirely new self—a self that is not identified with the habit."

Mastering Power-Thinking

It is a bright day when a man or woman sees the need for thinking with full force. Far too many people think loosely, mechanically, without design or purpose. They fail to realize that the mind possesses dozens of self-serving powers, such as *attention* and *flexibility*.

The chief enemy of power-thinking is habit. People think along the same lines day after day without realizing that habitual thought has limited benefits. Habitual thinking is circle-thinking that leads nowhere. It blocks mental exploration, it prevents a man from searching out and finding higher levels of living.

The first step in venturing beyond mechanical thinking is to become aware that we are doing just that. We must not mistake an echo for an answer. This supplies our first clue to an alternative; we sense that there is something superior to mechanical thought.

It is known that the famous Cullinan diamond is only one half of the original stone. By studying the inner structure of this fabulous gem, scientists know that it has another half, undiscovered as yet. A man's mind is like that. We need the mechanical part all right, for it releases us from consciously thinking about routine matters, like walking or dressing. But the other half, the creative part, is also necessary if we are to live more than a merely mechanical life. We must find and put to use the other half of our mental diamond. [MENTAL PICTURE 25]

One way to engage in power-thinking is to *think from a basic principle of truth*. Consider this principle as sort of a camp from which you will explore the forest of life. Select a Mental Picture from this book that attracts you in particular. Give it your consistent attention and interest. Let your mind explore it as you go through your day. Try to find its deeper meaning. This kind of easy-going reflection permits the principle to unfold itself, to tell you its full story. And that, in turn, raises your living-level.

Dissolving Destructive Habits

"Why," asked someone, "do we repeat our self-defeating behavior? For instance, bad temper. Why would a man cling to such a destructive habit for year after year?"

"We cling to self-defeating habits because we don't really see them as such. Remember the basic principle that no man ever *consciously* harms himself. We cling to harmful habits because they give us temporary gratification of some kind. A man might justify his bad temper because he thinks it makes him look like a man of strength, like someone who knows his rights and demands them. This justification smothers his ability to recognize bad temper as a self-destructive habit."

"How would he become aware of his self-deception?"

"By willingly dropping the imaginary self-picture he has of being a strong and dominating individual. As he does so, he becomes natural, and has no further need for temper. He was using it to support his fictitious picture of strength. But no longer having that picture, he no longer needs to hang it on the nail of temper."

"Then this man must start observing himself? He must see that he is acting out a false role?"

"Exactly. Then, his self-observation will cause him to challenge that false self-picture. That in itself is fine progress; he has already weakened its hold on him. Along with this, the man begins to think along new lines. He says to himself, 'Let's see, now, this negative behavior of mine is really getting me nowhere. I always end up scared and miserable. *This must be self-defeating behavior*. Yes, that's what it is. And I don't want to go on with it any longer.' "

"It seems so easy when you explain it, but why do we so stubbornly persist in the wrong way?"

"Because of another false assumption we have—that the present self-damaging way is the *only* way. It isn't the only way, for there is the great alternative of inner freedom. But a man in mental prison can't see the outside world; he knows only prison. He will even resist you if you tell him of liberty."

"Why?"

"He fears that the loss of prison means the loss of himself. He thinks he will be lost, empty, with no place to go. His prison-conditioned mind reasons, 'Better to be miserable than to be homeless.' He doesn't realize that there is a castle for him."

"We find this castle by challenging our conditioned outlooks?"

"Yes. Learn to see that they are merely conditioned attitudes. But do so light-heartedly. You can work hard without making it hard work. Have fun with the adventure, for that's what it is— an adventure in self-discovery."

Why Listening to Messages Helps Break Habits

Get the habit of closely examining your unprofitable experiences. Discover how they came about. Study the causes that produced the effect. Make it a scientific investigation. The answer to an unhappy experience is hidden within the experience itself.

Most importantly, discover the role that you played in bringing about the result. Don't hesitate to take responsibility for your personal part. Self-honesty leads to self-insight. Self-insight leads to freedom from negative habits.

All self-examination should be done unemotionally. Don't blame yourself or dislike yourself for anything. Self-blame only creates new waves of unprofitable emotions. Instead, look at the experience with a calm and curious mind. Remember that your objective is not to find fault with anything, but to scientifically look at the event with profit as your goal.

It helps to examine an unrewarding experience in the way that a wise cook might look over a cake recipe that didn't turn out so well. The cook wouldn't get angry at either himself or the recipe, rather, he would study the entire process. He would review the ingredients, check the oven temperature, and so on. That would break up the previous negative process.

Whenever we experience physical discomfort, like a headache, that discomfort is really a message. It tries to tell us something *for our own good*. It might inform us that we are involved in too many needless activities. It might signal that resentment is a wrong reaction to being ignored by someone. If heeded, that message can help us make corrections.

The same with upsetting experiences. We should again listen to the message. So, consider this idea the next time something bothers you. It will help you to think toward the experience in a new way—a non-distressing way.

To summarize, we should let negative events show us where we are out of harmony with natural laws of living. As Francis Bacon wrote, "Nature is commanded by obeying her."

Learn from an experience by examining that experience. That is how to exchange poor life-habits for rich ones.

FOREMOST FEATURES OF THIS CHAPTER

1. All unwanted habits can be replaced with beneficial ones.
2. Do not identify with an unwanted habit. It is something merely acquired; it is not a part of the real you.
3. Increase your receptivity to Mental Pictures. Let them work for you more and more.
4. Your thinking habits determine the kind of life you lead.
5. Do not resist new truths. They want to set you free.
6. Lift your level of awareness.
7. Everything good happens to you as you switch your life-habits from negative to positive. Prove it for yourself!
8. You are tied to a sad past by mental chains only. Break them.
9. Do not try to change a habit with a direct attack. Your total understanding causes it to fall away.
10. Listen to the secret message of your experiences. Let them help you build self-serving habits.

5

The New Way to
Command Other People

"Why is it," asked Philip R., "that my relations with other people are so painful? Regardless of the methods I use, nothing goes right—at least, not for long. Honestly, now, is there a right way?"

This chapter answers Philip's question. The methods you will meet, I am sure, are entirely different from anything you have ever encountered before. And they will work differently—far more effectively—than previous methods. You are in for some profitable surprises.

There are definite psychological laws governing human relationships. As they are understood and applied, they change these relationships into what you want them to be. If you persistently practice, you cannot fail. Brightness will appear in your home life, in handling children, socially, in contacts with the opposite sex, in business—everywhere. Just as Spring turns everything green, so do these laws refresh every area of human relations.

We start with that all-powerful principle that threads in and out of Psycho-Pictography:

To change others, first change yourself.

Let's take an everyday situation and see how it works:

Philip R., who asked the previous question, became more specific by saying, "I have a trapped feeling when I'm with other people. I'm ill at ease; don't know what to say. I wonder whether I'm liked and approved by others. What about this trapped feeling?"

"Forget other people. Work with your own mind."

"How?"

"This trapped feeling springs from your need of approval. You want them to like you, but you're not sure that they will. From now on, Philip, don't seek their approval; don't try so hard to please. Simply go about your business and be done with it. Be courteous, but don't sacrifice your inner integrity by asking for their approval. This is not selfishness. It's the finding of your True Self."

Philip later reported, "It's strange. By having a better attitude toward myself, other people act better toward me. Why didn't I see this years ago?"

If you ever have a trapped feeling when with others, you can free yourself with these principles.

Practice Self-Study

Self-change starts with self-study. But self-study presents a problem to some people, usually expressed like this:

"I can see some value in self-examination and self-knowledge, but doesn't it lead to gloom and self-centeredness? Shouldn't we try to forget ourselves?"

We must reverse our position entirely on this.

The right kind of self-study cannot lead to self-centeredness. The fact is, genuine self-observation is the very power that frees us from self-absorption. *The whole purpose of self-study is inner freedom through self-knowledge.* We can only forget ourselves as we understand ourselves. Lack of self-study keeps us imprisoned. Self-knowledge is the key for escape.

Motive is everything. We must have correct reasons for examining our inner life. Merely to worry or fret over ourselves is the very opposite of self-observation. They are not only painful in themselves but they make the snarl even worse.

The correct motive for self-study is just one thing—*self-under-standing*. That is what we need. That is why we work on ourselves. To become free, we must see what holds us in bondage. If we want to be happier, we must know what inner barriers block that higher state. If we need more poise and strength, we must learn how to draw them out of our natural resources.

As for forgetting ourselves, this is impossible until we first heal ourselves. A wounded soldier is compelled to think of his wound until it heals.

The right kind of self-study is prompted by a desire for inner healing. Our sincere purpose must be to exchange negative patterns for positive ones. We must want to be self-aware men and women. The story goes about the man who tumbled down a flight of stairs, making a loud racket. Picking himself up, he asked, "I wonder what all the noise was about?" That man hadn't enough self-awareness to see the cause of the noise. But we can do much better. Sincere self-study reveals that many of our annoying noises are within ourselves. Seeing that, we will soon cease bothering ourselves.

To summarize: Study yourself for entirely practical purposes. Plunge into the game with the intention of seeing that *there is an entirely superior way to live your life.*

Discover Your Own Temple of Diana

Some years ago an Englishman named J. T. Wood was seized by an ambition. He wanted to discover the ancient and long-lost Temple of Diana. Its discovery would be a landmark in archeology, for the magnificent temple was one of the seven wonders of the ancient world. So the British Museum sent him out to make the search at Ephesus, a former city of Greece.

Wood encountered one difficulty after another. As time passed, money ran short. Rain and mud bogged down the search. Workmen proved unreliable. Wood was personally attacked by an assassin, but escaped. Worst of all was the deep dismay over the lack of results. Their persistent probes revealed no sign of Diana's fabulous temple.

But Wood possessed a dynamic character trait: He wanted results badly enough! He had no thought but to actually discover what he knew was there.

And he did. On New Year's Day, a spade struck a pavement

of white marble. That first clue was all Wood needed. He surprised and delighted the world with his discovery of the beautiful Temple of Diana. [MENTAL PICTURE 26]

That is the sort of ambition we must have. We must want badly enough actually to find what we suspect is there.

In this instance we want to discover the secrets of human behavior. We search to uncover people as they really are, not as we merely believe or hope they are. In following sections we will expose some unprofitable thinking toward other people.

Whenever you want wealthy discoveries about human nature —your own or others—remember this wise observation:

> *You may be always successful if you do but set out well, and let your thoughts and practice proceed upon right method. Let not the genuine value of anything escape you.* (Marcus Aurelius)

Should You Help Others?

People confess, "I'm confused over the duty of helping other people. I want to be good to others, but I just don't have the strength. Is this selfish of me?"

A false sense of duty damages human harmony. So if you have ever asked a similar question, please follow:

For now, don't concern yourself in the least with ideas about helping others. Here is one of the sorriest traps ever invented. For one thing, it is necessary to discover what is really helpful to others.

Concentrate your strength on achieving the self-change we have been covering. *This is your first duty.* In the long run, it is the richest contribution you could ever make to others.

Don't try to *do something* for another, rather, try to *be someone* to him. This other person, whether spouse or child or friend, will then inwardly recognize that you are different; they will sense your inner strength; they will have you as an example of a mature and unafraid person. You will be the genuinely spiritual person whom they hoped existed after all. You will be the one for whom they have been searching all their lives, and the one who can *really* help them. All they have found up to now is someone who did something for them in expectation of getting something in return. But you, with your True Self in command, are different. Everyone secretly knows that you can only love someone when you don't want something from him. And that is the kind of genuine love you have to offer.

The above question indicates a false sense of guilt. This guilt is caused by trying to reconcile what you *were told* was your duty and what your inner self *knows* is true about the whole matter of helping others. The truth is, you are not required to help others until you are able to do so without consciously thinking about it. Then, your aid will be spontaneous, something you naturally want to do.

It's like a young peach tree. It makes no deliberate effort to give peaches, for it knows it has nothing as yet to give. It knows that its present task is to harmonize with natural laws of growth by taking in sunshine and air. Then, in the right time, it effortlessly produces peaches for others to enjoy. [MENTAL PICTURE 27]

How to Become a Superior Person

You need never deliberately *try* to do anything for another. If it is a conscious effort, it will be painful to you, useless to the other person, and wrong for both of you. You need only put first things first. The first thing is your own inner enrichment. Do this, and you will never again be bothered about when or how you should help others. You will be in that state of inner freedom where you help others not by *doing something,* but by *being someone.*

This, then, is the perfect method: *To change others, first change yourself.*

There is something different, something really remarkable about the man or woman who has accomplished great inner change, who has found the True Self. You have probably had the interesting experience of meeting someone who impressed you as having uncommon inner strength.

Such a unique person has a look of quietness that bears no resemblance to the calm-appearing mask that many people wear. He doesn't try to make an impression. He can be honest with you because he doesn't want anything from you. He is close to you, yet at the same time, has an air of detachment. Such a superior personality is excellently described by Professor Burtt:

> *"Love of detachment," on the other hand, is free from all demandingness, all need to control the loved one, all dependence upon him. It is detached, not in the sense of withdrawing from emotional concern for others, but in the sense of gladly accepting them as they are, not requiring them to be different from their present selves as the price on one's friendly affection. It is detached, not from caring for others, but from preoccupation with oneself, and from the need to make others serve the cravings of the self. It is the compassionate giving of oneself to the world without asking for anything in return . . .[1]*

Genuine kindness is not what we *do*. It is what we *are*.

How to Handle a Difficult Person

As you have discovered, the objective of Mental Pictures is to teach you to view everything differently. This is the magic that changes everything into what it should be. There is something within you that responds to this truth; for deep down, every man senses that his mental viewpoints make his world whatever it is.

During World War II, the Aldis lamp was used with valuable results. It was a signalling lamp with a special feature. When flashed from a ship, it could be seen only by someone standing within a certain stretch of the shoreline. Anyone standing too far on either side of the stretch could not see it. But anyone wanting to catch the message, needed only to change his viewpoint. [MENTAL PICTURE 28]

Now, I want to give you a valuable viewpoint to use in all your human relations. It is really a miracle method for handling people, especially those who make it difficult for you.

The method is simplicity itself: Whenever encountering a troublesome person, do not identify him as being cruel or stupid or rude or anything else like that. Instead, *see him as a frightened*

[1] Edwin A. Burtt, *Man Seeks the Divine* (New York: Harper and Row, Publishers, Incorporated, 1957).

person. This is exactly what the cruel or rude person is. All negative emotions have a foundation of fear. An individual displays these negativities to the degree that he is afraid. His angry aggressiveness is the only method he presently knows for releasing the tension of fear.

Now let's see how your switch in viewpoint changes things.

Suppose that when first meeting this difficult person you do take the wrong viewpoint of seeing him as cruel or hateful. This will have a definite effect on the way you try to handle him. It will make *you* afraid of *him,* for negativity in one person arouses negativity in another. So if you turn negative toward this other person, you cannot handle him wisely and tactfully.

But see what happens when you really understand that he acts as he does because he is scared. This will not make you negative in turn. It does not make you angry or defensive. *You remain emotionally free of him.* So you are able to proceed calmly and wisely. Not only that, but your calmness impresses him; your strength is transferred to him. The process is reversed. Instead of his negativity transferring itself to you, you transfer your positiveness to him! It is much like offering a new kind of candy to a child; he may not understand it at first, but he senses that you are his friend. In time, he may taste that candy—your understanding of him—and the relationship is magically transformed.

Try this miracle method for yourself in a specific relationship, perhaps in your business or home. It is really remarkable what changes it makes. As an extra benefit, you will prove something that you have suspected all along—that when you *see* things correctly, correct results occur.

Why People Treat You as They Do

Let's take another area of human relations and see why self-strength is so essential.

Have you ever wondered why people treat you as they do? The answer may surprise you, but what a rich revelation!

Whenever you meet another person, your behavior tells him how to treat you. By *behavior* we mean everything about you that is observed by the other person. Your facial expressions flash signals indicating either strength or weakness. Gestures, postures, and your manner of walk are definite signs as to your character and personality. What you say and how you say it convey certain impressions to your observer. If your eyes wander during a conversation, he draws certain conclusions—perhaps that you are disinterested in him. You flash hundreds of impressions by which the other man sizes you up.

People are far more alert to you than they appear to be. This alertness leads them to ask, "What kind of a person is he? How must I treat him in order to get along?"

Now we come to the vital point: Your over-all behavior creates an impression of either strength or weakness. If it is weak or negative, he will not warm up to you. No one likes weakness in another person, for it reminds the observer of his own weakness. What he dislikes in himself he dislikes in others. Also, if he senses weakness, he tends to take advantage of it. This is an unfortunate truth about some people. So you cannot afford an impression of weakness or negativity.

As you develop inwardly, as you raise your level of awareness, it changes the way you appear to others. You need do nothing to force this exterior change; in fact, there is nothing you can do by working from the outside. Strength proceeds from the inner to the outer. As your inner self develops more power, it automatically expresses itself in every form of exterior behavior. People then see you as a different person, for that is exactly what you are! Then, they treat you with new respect.

You attract what you are. This is an absolute law of human relations. It works in your favor as you work with it. Your part is to build a strong inner self that expresses itself outwardly. Do this and you will never again worry over your treatment by others.

How Understanding Can Protect You From Cruelty

What should be your state of mind toward a person in your life who is definitely cruel?

There is only one way of thinking that serves your best interest. But what a marvelous way!

Understanding.

If you understand, if you really understand a cruel or revengeful or vicious person, you are entirely free of that person. He or she cannot hurt you in any way whatsoever. When you have insight into a negative individual you do not then project your own negative emotions toward him. *It is not his cruelty that hurts; it is your own negative reaction that hurts.* But when you dwell on a high level of awareness, you do not react in fear or anger or agony toward that cruel person.

Suppose you see a tiger in a zoo. Now, you know very well that this tiger is a cruel and vicious animal. He would destroy you if he could. You understand his ferocity, yet you are unafraid of him; his cruelty does not alarm you. Why are you fearless? Because you know he is powerless to harm you. The bars protect you. [MENTAL PICTURE 29]

Do likewise with a cruel person. Understand his cruelty, but do not personalize it. He has absolutely no power to touch you. Just as a tiger is restrained by the bars, a hostile person is prevented from harming you *by your own understanding of him.* Your insight makes firm bars. But if you personalize, if you get emotional, if you unthinkingly attribute power to that person, you weaken the bars. Then, you yourself permit him to spring at you. You may believe that the other person's cruelty is your problem; it is not. The problem is that you weaken the bars of your perception. But if you will work at building your understanding, no one can ever hurt you.

Think about this.

Don't Make This Mistake

I want to tell you about the single greatest mistake anyone makes when estimating the character of another person. It will help you avoid mistakes in your relations with others. It is especially helpful when meeting someone for the first time. The single greatest mistake a person makes is this: He wrongly assumes that the other person is as mature and reasonable and considerate as he appears to be on the surface.

Do you have any idea of the shock and grief caused by this false assumption? Perhaps you know from personal experience.

We don't see below the surface of the other person. Instead, we idealize, we paint him with the qualities we need and want him to have. Then, when the paint wears thin, we are shocked at what we see underneath. If the other man smiles a lot, we assume that he has a cheerful personality, while he really smiles from mechanical habit. If he displays a decisive manner, we believe he is sure of himself, while his very manner is a cover-up for inner uncertainty.

You must remember that other people have far greater inner conflicts and confusions than they reveal. You sometimes see these suppressed pressures burst through with a flash of anger, sarcasm, or accusation.

Self-understanding helps us to see and understand other people. By being aware of our own inner selves, we become perceptive in our judgments of others and wise in our relations.

Simple understanding has no fear. Don't just project your ideals onto others; don't see them as you hope they are. Don't let your mind trick you. Remember, mental suffering is a clash between illusion and reality. Don't project the illusion and you won't hear a crash. Here is a simple system: Don't see the other man as *you* *think* he is; let *him* gradually reveal what he *really* is.

Use these ideas wherever you meet people. They will give you a new and calm command.

Wearing Your Own Magic Moccasins

There is a legend about the Indian tribe that feared to search for food in a nearby forest. The forest was dark, forbidding, unmarked by trails. Even the boldest of warriors were often lost for days. Along came a medicine man offering magic moccasins. Whoever wore a pair was surely and safely guided back to camp. [MENTAL PICTURE 30]

The following brief points are like magic moccasins. They guarantee safe guidance through the forest of people. To walk safely, wear them!

1. The most persuasive power you have toward others is a mature self.
2. The mark of greatness is to be superior without feeling superior.
3. "The consciousness of being loved softens the keenest pang." (Joseph Addison)

4. The turning point in all your exterior relations comes when you start changing your inner self.
5. Strong people attract the weak.
6. Possessiveness and dependency are not states of love.
7. Your own level of being attracts the kind of people who enter your life.
8. "He is happy as well as great who needs neither to obey nor command in order to be something." (Goethe)
9. Your True Self cannot be afraid of anyone.
10. You break the cord of painful thought toward another person by snipping the connection within your own mind.
11. It is very painful to pretend to be someone.
12. Any sincere effort at bettering your human relations returns a reward.
13. Don't drain your energy by thinking negatively toward people who harm you.
14. You get along with others to the exact degree that you get along with yourself.
15. A real person stands out like a man among statues.

How to Avoid Hurt Feelings

Before ending this chapter, I want to emphasize the importance of seeing the difference between the True Self and the False Self. You will profit richly by reviewing the section in Chapter 2 on this. But let's now take a practical example. It will show you the magical power of the True Self.

"How," people often ask, "can I avoid getting my feelings hurt so easily and so often?" Let's see how the True Self accomplishes this.

Picture in your mind the following scene: Two men are standing outdoors in fair weather. One of them is a magician with supernormal powers; the other is an average man.

Suddenly, a storm strikes. Rain and wind whip furiously around the men. The average man, caught in that storm, gets knocked around, soaked. He becomes helplessly miserable.

But the magician! That's another story. He has the power to make himself invisible. So, as the storm breaks, that's what he does. In becoming an invisible man he cannot be touched

by rain or wind. *His invisibility gives the storm nothing whatsoever to strike.* How can a storm strike an invisible man? It
can't. It passes on through. The magician remains calm, undis-
turbed, unhurt. [MENTAL PICTURE 31]

You have power to become such a magician. And you have it
now.

There is only one way in the entire world to avoid the pain of
being offended, insulted, accused, attacked, hurt. And this is it.

The magician is your True Self which you now possess.

Ask Yourself This Question

Please understand all this. It is the False Self—the average man
of Mental Picture 31—that always gets insulted and cheated and
wronged. It is the self that gets hurt by the storm of sarcastic remarks and cruel actions of other people.

But the True Self can never be hurt by anyone or anything.
The storm passes right on through.

So ask yourself, "Which self do these outer storms fall upon?"
If they fall on the False Self, with all its prides and sensitivities,
you get your feelings hurt. If they fall on the True Self, they pass
on through. The False Self is a solid block that gets hit by everything, but the invisible True Self stops nothing.

Work at dissolving the False Self.

I assure you that all this is not some vague theory and is not
mere words. It is one of the most practical ideas you could ever
understand. French novelist Honoré de Balzac was right when
he declared, "Miracles are within us—natural facts which some
call supernormal." He was just as right when he added, "None
are superior to what you might become."

KEEP THESE IDEAS IN MIND

1. The plans in this chapter give you a new and effective
   command in all your human relations.
2. Understand and work with the natural laws governing
   relations with others.

3. For smoothness in human affairs, see people as they really are, not as you may want them to be.
4. The most valuable contribution you can make to others is to be inwardly strong. They need your strength.
5. An understanding of the other person gives you skill and power with him.
6. Your over-all action and behavior tells others how to treat you. Work with this idea.
7. No one can hurt your feelings unless you react in hurt. Don't.
8. Remember, other people have many more problems and conflicts than appear on the surface.
9. Review the 15 points following Mental Picture 30.
10. When you find your True Self, all your human relations are cheery and effective.

6

How to Set Up Your
Own Success Program

Success? Exactly what *is* success? That, obviously, is the first intelligent inquiry we want to make.

You are successful when you really enjoy your life.

There can be no other genuine definition. It digs right to the root of things. A man might make lots of money or get elected to public office or be popular at his club, but what good is all that unless he really enjoys himself? It is of no use whatsoever—and every man and woman inwardly knows it.

The great achievement and the high moral duty of every individual is to be happy through realization of Spiritual Laws.

History records how the ancient islanders of Polynesia studied the flights of sea-birds. Over the days and weeks they observed the great flocks fly away from their home islands to disappear over the distant ocean. Those daring sea-birds provided a valuable clue to the islanders. They reasoned that somewhere, beyond their present sight, rested new and fruitful islands to be claimed. They acted upon that clue. Setting out in their frail canoes, they followed the seasonal flights. They finally found what they suspected was out there—new islands, ready for abundant living. [MENTAL PICTURE 32]

That is what we will do in this chapter. We will follow the clues to a more successful land for living.

Always Put First Things First

People say, "When it comes to success, I never know what I want. One minute it's one thing and the next minute something entirely different. How can I get logical order in my searchings?"

Put first things first.

The first things are always those related to our inner life. Secondary goals are the outward ones, such as our financial activities and our material possessions. By placing the inner life first, we then enjoy the outer! Why not enjoy *yourself* as well as your possessions? This simple thought rarely occurs to millions of intelligent people.

There is nothing wrong with having lots of money; it is just more important to have lots of inner quietness. It is a good idea to redecorate your home; but a far better idea to redecorate the way you think. It is interesting to know the news of the day; it is ten times more interesting to know yourself.

People hesitate to set first things first. It is because they don't realize that inner success is what they *really* want. They fail to see that exterior things are useless substitutes for inner success. A man often achieves a financial fortune and then is surprised to find that he is really no happier than before. Even this shock doesn't wake him up to the fact that his values are all wrong, that he has placed last things first. He usually goes on to a second false assumption: he assumes that some *other* exterior achievement— perhaps fame or power—will do it. But they never will do it. The outer can never do anything for the inner.

It takes genuine daring and courage to set first things first. And it takes a practical mind. People often tell me, "But Mr. Howard, this is a practical world; we must live in a practical way."

True. It is for that very reason that a man must place his inner riches first! Then—and then only—can he place his exterior affairs in their proper places. And that is when he begins to *enjoy* his success as well as *achieve* it. Let's go into details with:

An Amazing Truth About Money

In reading this book, which plunges deeply into the inner world of man, you may have a question. This question frequently comes up, especially among businessmen. It is a profitable inquiry with an exciting answer. It goes like this:

"I certainly see the need for exploring my inner world of thoughts and emotions. After all, a man's life is much more than his material possessions. He also lives in his invisible world of desires and sympathies and affections. But I wonder about something. Should we spend too much time in this inner world? Isn't the outer world the practical one? After all, as a salesman, it's vital that I concentrate on profits, sales, customers, and other tangible items.

"To sum up my question, what can all these psychological ideas do for me in my commercial world? What is their value? Why should I study them intensely? I'm sincere about this. I really want to know."

If you have ever asked this question, an amazing truth is about to enter your mind. Welcome it heartily. I guarantee a wealthy reward in everything you do, including your business life of profits, sales, and customers.

Listen!

There is not a single idea in this entire book that doesn't connect directly with your financial affairs. And that connection is favorable to you in a way you cannot presently imagine. But just wait!

Obviously, your inward feelings affect your outward acts of business. If you are sad and depressed, you rob yourself of energies that might otherwise be used for winning new customers. If you fear your business rivals, that fear overhangs like a dark cloud, darkening your business day.

But look at the positive side! Your inner cheeriness naturally shines outwardly upon everyone you meet, creating a sunny business climate. If you have inner patience and kindness, others will sense that and will want to be with you.

Nothing is more important for a businessman to understand than the absolute connection between his inner, psychological life and his outer, commercial life.

A toy top with inward balance spins merrily, to the delight of the child who sees it. Likewise, as the great psychological truths maintain our inner stability, we spin merrily in every exterior activity, including our business affairs.

I want to give you a superb example of all we have been talking about. It is the report of Larry D., a junior executive in the insurance business:

> I was at work one morning when an idea flashed through my mind. It concerned the difference between the True Self and the False Self. You had made it clear that the False Self causes all our trouble. It is touchy, defensive, and everything else harmful. Anyway, I wondered how soon I'd have a chance to turn this knowledge into practical experience.
>
> It came a few hours later. Driving back from lunch, I saw that someone had taken my reserved parking space. I was annoyed. I felt like telling him off. That was my first reaction to that impudent car. I hotly asked what right it had to take *my* reserved place.
>
> Then I had a second thought. I asked exactly *why* I felt so resentful. Here I made a fascinating discovery, the very kind you tell us about. It was my *False Self* that was offended. I clearly saw how this vain and petty little self was robbing my peace of mind. And just for the sake of a stupid little parking space!
>
> What a revelation! For the very first time in my life I saw how I could react peacefully to any exterior event. I need *not* be at the mercy of the egotistical False Self. My True Self can take that very same parking event with a simple quietness. Let me repeat—what a fantastic revelation to see that I could react in a *totally different way*. And what a relief!
>
> You know what helped this insight? A funny thing. There was an open parking space next to my office door, while my reserved space was farther away. I could have had that open space. That proved that my resentful reaction had nothing to do with practical matters. My petty vanity was hurt at someone taking *my* space.
>
> You know, Mr. Howard, you've been trying to get this into our heads for a long time. Thanks for your patience. You were calmly waiting for us to see what you knew to be the truth.

I wish every businessman could see it. Believe me, I'll do my part to tell them.

For the very first time, I see the truth we have reviewed so often—the truth that our viewpoints make our world whatever it is. A new awareness creates an entirely new world.

So it is. It is a world where you can be fully involved with life, but never hurt by it.

If you ever ask, "Are psychological and spiritual ideas of practical value in the business world?" I want you to know:

Nothing—absolutely nothing—is more practical.

For better business, and enjoyable business, you cannot afford to overlook them. Not only will they solve business problems, but they do something far superior to that: they prevent problems from arising in the first place. Here is the mark of the truly wise man· his insight prevents problems from ever appearing in the first place.

Relate every idea in Psycho-Pictography to your everyday experiences, including your money-making affairs. You will see how wonderfully practical they are.

Always Remember Your Castle

People remark, "I get discouraged so easily. Suppose I set up my success program but lose my drive. How can I zoom ahead once more?"

A king was out hunting with his princes in a forest many miles from the castle. A sudden snowstorm fell on the party. In the confusion, the king was separated from the others. When he failed to return to the castle after four days he was given up as lost. But on the fifth day, he appeared in the warm dining room. Someone asked him how he had found strength enough to keep going. The king replied, "I remembered all that the castle means to me." [MENTAL PICTURE 33]

That kind of thinking will keep anyone going forward. Even while involved in difficulties and obstacles, we can remember what it means to succeed. This remembrance creates a powerful emotional force that carries us through.

It is helpful to concentrate on some specific castle, that is, some special goal of yours. Examples:

> To be less tense and anxious
> To build a brighter future
> To banish depression
> To be a better businessman
> To have smoother human relations.

Think of what it means to win one of these. Remember the rewards that go with your success. This supplies strength that keeps you going all the way to your castle.

You are wiser than you think. You sometimes catch a flash of insight that reveals the truth about things. This flash, coming at an unexpected moment, proves that the truth is already within you and known very well by you. It waits only for your quiet invitation. It is this brief brightness—this Magnificent Glimpse —that is the foundation for all genuine enthusiasm. "A thrill passes through all men at the reception of a new truth . . ." (Emerson)

Pursue this thrill. It is the only enthusiasm that will never wear away, that will never disappoint you. If you will simply permit its intensity to grow, it will do so naturally. Then, you will know an excitement toward life that you have never known before. It is like observing a beautiful sunset: gradually, as the colors rise and spread, they carry you inwardly aloft; you are eager to experience the greater beauty that you know is only a matter of time.

The Secret of Lasting Will-Power

People often tell me, "For many years, I've tried and failed to use my will-power. Does will-power really exist? If so, how can I find it?"

Yes, will-power certainly exists, but unless a man achieves a degree of inner unity he cannot awaken it from its sleeping state. To say the same thing in positive fashion, by winning a measure of self-unity, a man finds a will to achieve his desires, whatever they may be. Such a man is living *his own life;* he is not at the mercy of his fickle False Self.

A man without inner unity is like a group of children at play. They decide to go on a hike, but can't agree on the direction to take. One child calls out for the others to follow him northward, so they all go north for a few yards. Then, a second child calls out that it would be better to go south, so they all switch to the new direction. Back and forth they go, first one way and then another, never getting anywhere. They finally give up in exhaustion and dismay. [MENTAL PICTURE 34]

A man has thousands of inner parts. He has an emotional center made up of all sorts of desires and inclinations, many of them in opposition to others. His mind contains a vast variety of thoughts and opinions and viewpoints, including negative and contradictory ones. As a man works on himself, say, through self-study, he gathers together all his positive parts into a working unit. These positive forces then harmonize consistently and for persistent purpose. The man becomes like an automobile engine whose parts are assembled into a power-plant capable of carrying the car wherever desired. Such a man has genuine will.

How to achieve this inner unity that supplies will-power? First, realize that it is quite possible for you to pull yourself together! Then, casually absorb all the Mental Pictures in this book. Your unity is their purpose.

Your Attractive Personality

What about personality? How does it enter your program for general success? And what, exactly, *is* personality?

Personality is the outer expression of what you inwardly are. (Please consider this fact to be like an iceberg—more beneath the surface than appears.) This being so, the wise man starts with inner alteration. Then, the outer self brightens naturally, effortlessly. Such improvements include attractive facial expressions, a pleasant voice, public poise, and much more.

Additionally, the conqueror of his inner world possesses a certain mystical charm. His inner self shines for all to see, like the cabin lights that glow on a passing ship in the night.

The single greatest force for creating a new personality is a full claim upon your personal integrity.

This means:

You must not do things for other people in an effort to make them like you.

You have no duty to accept any idea as true until you have personally proven it.

You must strike out toward freedom from all forms of fear and anxiety.

You should take a cheerful responsibility for releasing your True Self.

You must not sacrifice your mind to another person merely because he seems sure of himself.

I am thinking of a boulevard merchant whose very quietness shouts of deep inner strength. Without saying a word, you sense his contact with the lofty life. I suspect that many a customer is unknowingly drawn to his shop because of this. Mysteriously—yet in a very real way—he transmits his secret strength to everyone around him.

The question came up, "Do you mean that we should work from the motive of attracting others?"

"No. A glittering personality that merely attracts others is not enough. Secret despair lies behind such shallowness. The mature personality attracts others, yet, at the same time, leaves the possessor contented. It is found by fully claiming your individual integrity."

How to Enjoy Your Voyage

You must not worry over your progress. Whether you sail toward a material goal or a psychological one, anxiety has absolutely no place in your plans. How can you break the connection between your mind and worry?

By enjoying the trip itself. By abandoning all ideas that you are responsible for keeping things going.

A young man found himself stranded in Japan. Thinking he might work his way back home on a merchant ship, he applied to the captain. His offer was accepted. On the sailing date he reported to the captain and asked, "What should I do?"

"Just enjoy the voyage," the captain answered.

"Enjoy the voyage?" repeated the puzzled young man.

"Yes. That's all you need to do. Your passage has already been paid."

It developed that a friend had heard of the problem and had paid the fare home. [MENTAL PICTURE 35]

Likewise, there is nothing we need to do or really can do except to enjoy the trip. As long as we are aboard the ship, that is, if we are traveling along with the right principles, we can completely relax. The ship is headed in the right direction, and so are we. Oh, yes, the voyage might include some stormy emotions for a while, or we may be rocked by mental confusions, but that is not really a problem. The Truth is always intact, and so are we.

We must rid our minds of the idea that we are responsible for results. That is a tremendous contribution to your sense of relaxation.

Make up your mind to enjoy the voyage. Sooner or later, your mind will agree that it's a great idea.

It is your moral duty to be happy.

Making the Perfect Start

Wherever you want to achieve a new success, you can make a perfect start. Whether in your business affairs or domestic life or mental world, you can make a start that ends successfully. The start of a new project needs close examination because it sometimes creates a mental crisis. People ask, "Where should I start?" and "How can I persist?" and "What should I do?"

I want to show you how to answer all these questions. Just follow as many of these rules as you can.

Whenever you start a new project:

1. Know exactly what you want.
2. Be confident of your inner forces.
3. Collect all available information.
4. Dismiss wasteful and negative attitudes.
5. Score a series of small successes.
6. Harmonize with natural laws of success.
7. Cease pointless actions.
8. Make the most of every opportunity.

9. Concentrate on one area at a time.
10. Enjoy your new project.

Suppose that you want to start a new program in your relations with other people. You want to understand people better. You wish to attract new friends, customers, associates. You desire to be more attractive to others. Well, you can get off to a good start with any or all of the above points.

Take point 3; why not begin a regular reading program with solid books of psychology and social relations? For point 6, you can review some of the natural laws of human relations from Chapter 5. Take point 9; why not concentrate on making your conversations of more interest to others?

Do you know why you can be at perfect peace with any new program? Because *life never requires you to do anything beyond your present ability*. Stop and think about that. You need to do only what you *can* do for now.

What can you do right now?

You can start!

How to Build Personal Strength

How can you build more personal strength with which to achieve either an inner or outer success?

All extra strength comes from additional self-unity. And self-unity is one purpose you have in using Mental Pictures. They help to unite your inner forces so that daily challenges turn into victories.

One benefit of self-unity is that you are totally engaged in the act of the moment, that is, your whole self is concentrated there. The opposite of this is a scattered mind. For instance, you may wish to relax, but your thoughts keep hopping away to some business matter. When the self-united man is relaxed he is like a cat dozing peacefully before the fireplace—he is in a mental state that knows nothing outside of itself. He doesn't merely feel relaxed; he *is* that state of relaxation.

Hannibal, the Carthaginian general, was once marching against Rome. He decided to enlist the aid of some neighboring tribes. He dispatched riders in a dozen directions with invitations to join him in the conquest of Rome. Some of the riders failed to persist in their search for the potential allies. Consequently, Hannibal never achieved the full power he might have had. [MENTAL PICTURE 36]

We must persist in our search for our hidden powers. They are there all right. We have already covered many of them, such as self-study and self-awareness. As we catch a glimpse of their willingness to help us, we readily enlist their aid. They then unite within us to make daily victories possible.

> *All our progress is an unfolding, like the vegetable bud. You have first an instinct, then an opinion, then a knowledge, as the plant has root, bud, and fruit. Trust the instinct to the end, though you can render no reason. It is vain to hurry it. By trusting it to the end, it shall ripen into truth and you shall know why you believe.* (Emerson)

Apply Three Magic Words and Succeed Where You Have Failed

What can be done whenever you feel that your best efforts are blocked? Is there a way to break into the clear again? There is.

In school we used to have a teacher who combined kindness with wisdom in order to help us. Whenever we ran into a classroom problem, she advised, "Try another way."

There is tremendous power in those three magic words!

That teacher knew, first of all, that there *was* an answer to the problem that baffled us. She also knew that we failed to find it because of our own wrong approach.

Likewise, there is an answer to every problem we may encounter. If it eludes us, we need to try another way. Maybe we need to follow *several* fresh trails, maybe we must abandon *many* false paths. But why not go ahead and have fun with it? Why not adventure forward until we find the true course? What's the matter with doing that? Why not? It can be an exciting adventure!

Knowledge of mental laws is always a new and helpful approach. Many of the letters crossing my desk testify to this. Many readers, seeking aid in their relations with the opposite sex, discovered this while reading my previous book, *SECRETS OF MENTAL*

MAGIC: How to Use Your Full Power of Mind. Here is a particularly helpful message:

> *If you are interested in a finer love life, you must not miss the significance of this mental law:*
> *We attract and hold a person of the other sex who dwells on the same general level that we ourselves occupy. Like attracts like. To attract someone on a higher level—which means that he or she will be a much nicer person—we need do only one thing: raise your own level.*

Do not resist a new approach. Dare to explore it. People timidly hold back because they fear there is nothing better than their present method. There *is* a better method, there *is* brighter success. But to get to the moon we must first put the earth at our backs.

Apply the three magic words: *Try another way.*

Use Your Powers Correctly

Many people do not understand their inner forces. This bewilderment produces unnecessary failure—for man was made for success. For instance, people do not understand why their emotions and their imaginations cause so much damage. They wonder whether this destruction can be stopped.

A humorous incident, reported in the newspaper, introduces the answer:

A recently-hired employee of a zoo was assigned the task of setting up some new signs. The signs were intended to direct visitors to the various animals. The inexperienced employee set up the signs all right, but pointed them in wrong directions. Visitors wanting to see the bears found themselves at the alligator pond. Children who thought they were on their way to the monkeys arrived at the camel yard.

Noticing his mistake, the employee quickly turned them around so that they pointed correctly. Now, everyone walked in the directions they desired. [MENTAL PICTURE 37]

Our inner forces are like those signs. There is really nothing wrong with them. It is just that we have pointed them in the wrong directions. We are making negative use of positive power.

There is nothing the matter with our emotions or imaginations. We need only turn them in the right directions. Then we will head toward our desired destinations in life.

Let's select, as an example, a sense of self-responsibility. We usually take only those responsibilities that we presently feel ourselves capable of taking. We fail to challenge ourselves to greater achievement. Yet, we can enlarge our inner powers by deliberately tackling a bit more responsibility than we presently feel capable of handling. A man must dare to reach slightly above himself. Such a man soon finds his capacity matching his reach. The law is this: The more we dare to do, the more we *can* do.

Whenever you experience a negative emotion, remember the last Mental Picture. Recall that your feelings can be turned around, pointed in the right directions. The right directions are those that lead to higher levels of daily living.

Watch Your Own Progress

Perhaps you say, "I am studying the principles of Psycho-Pictography with you. Will I actually see myself thinking and acting in a new and better way? If so, how does it all come about?"

This hits upon one of the vital purposes of Psycho-Pictography: *Change. Self-change.* It always happens whenever you sincerely apply yourself. Self-change, a fresh way of thinking, is a great aim of Mental Pictures. It is an aim we must not miss.

It is strange how a person can study a truthful system for many years, perhaps attend countless classes, and yet remain the same kind of person inwardly. Such a person has missed the entire point—that of inner transformation. Such a man may be uneasy over the fact that he still has the same old worries and pains, but he never stops to ask himself *why* he remains in the same old rut. He must wake up and challenge himself.

It is not enough to hear the truth. We must openly receive it. The great clue is *receptivity*. Then, the received truth sets us free. It changes us. We become new. And so do our circumstances.

You can actually see yourself change for the better. It is observable magic. This change is seen by comparison. You discern that you are less anxious today than you were yesterday. You see definite improvement in the way you meet a crisis. You behave in a different and superior manner.

Suppose you decide to walk up the stairs of a ten-story building. You pause at the fifth floor to look out the window. At this fifth-story level, you can see a certain amount of the city. When you climb to the tenth floor, you see much more. You know that you are in a superior position because you can compare the two levels. Because you have changed your position, you increase the amount of the city to be enjoyed. This is observable success. [MENTAL PICTURE 38]

As you work with Psycho-Pictography, you will see actual changes. Incidents that formerly upset you will lose their negative power. Vague apprehensions will give way to tranquility. You will see, perhaps for the first time, that everything is really all right.

SPECIAL SECRETS FOR SUCCESS

1. What is success? First and last, it is personal happiness.
2. Place first things first. Success follows.
3. Nothing is of more practical value to you in your everyday business than psychological principles.
4. Connect the ideas of Psycho-Pictography to every area of your life. They are best friends.
5. You are wiser than you think. As we rid our minds of false notions, wisdom springs up like an underground stream.
6. Self-unity is self-power.
7. Review the ideas in this chapter about your personality. Let them enrich you.
8. Do not burden yourself with worry over results. Enjoy your voyage toward your goal.
9. Remember the three magic words: *Try another way.*
10. Self-change guarantees success.

7

How to Lose Inferiority and Win Self-Confidence

"What makes me act the way I do?"

That is a highly profitable question. Have you ever asked yourself what makes you act, feel, respond, and decide the way you do? Your investigation of this question will return immense rewards. The answer is, you act as you do because of the ideas that you think *from*. A timid thought projects a timid action or a frightened feeling. A decisive thought is the springboard from which purposeful action launches itself.

Learn this secret: The ideas *from which you think* are the springboards that make your life whatever it is. By changing these ideas, by thinking from a higher level, you uplift your entire life. Here is one of those absolute truths you need have no hesitation in accepting and working with wholeheartedly.

You have probably seen those divers down in Mexico who plunge from a tall cliff into the churning sea. In their original search for a proper diving position they covered and rejected several possibilities. One position was too low, another failed to offer enough clearance, a third was rejected because of the shallow sea at the point of a diver's entry. But at last they found a high pinnacle from which to dive with safety and skill. By launching themselves from this proper position, their high-diving succeeded. [MENTAL PICTURE 39]

That is what we must do also. We must launch our daily actions *from correct mental positions*. If we do not do so, we have neither safety nor success. But with them, we achieve a confidence that guarantees right results.

What are some of these confidence-building ideas from which you can act? We have already covered many of them up to this point in the book, but here are five more solid mental positions from which to think:

1. *The True Self is not subject to depression.*
2. *Mental Pictures enrich you.*
3. *All negative emotions can be dissolved.*
4. *Sincere work on yourself is always rewarded.*
5. *There is a way out!*

From this day forward, think *from* positive ideas like these. By doing so, you will not fail to change whatever things in your life you want to change.

Are You Climbing Mountains?

As you know, a pantomime drama is one in which most of the stage properties are imaginary. This idea introduces us to an impressive Mental Picture.

Picture a pantomimist on stage. He tries to climb a mountain by pulling himself upward on imaginary ropes. Now, as long as he is only pretending to climb, the non-existent ropes serve nicely. Since it is only a stage act, as long as he really doesn't want to climb, those imaginary ropes are fine.

But suppose that that same pantomimist went to a real mountain which he wanted to climb. Suppose he *then* used imaginary ropes. That would be foolish. He would get no-where. To make *real* progress, he needs to use *real* ropes. [MENTAL PICTURE 40]

Unfortunately, many people are doing this very thing. They try to use imaginary thought-ropes to climb real mountains. It just doesn't work. It is useless to try to reach a higher level of happiness by climbing with unrealistic thought-ropes. We need the real thing.

Let's look at the difference between imaginary and real thought-ropes:

Imaginary: I have no inner strength.
Real: You possess vast power you don't see as yet.
Imaginary: It's a frightening world.
Real: Your True Self knows no fear whatsoever.
Imaginary: I'm torn between one frantic desire and the next.
Real: Inner stability comes with self-understanding.

How can you tell whether a particular thought-rope is real or imaginary?

Put it to the practical test. Ask whether or not it lifts you to higher happiness, or whether you remain on a low level of anxiety. Be ruthlessly honest about it. This takes courage, but why not be a hero? If it works, it's real; if it fails, it's imaginary.

Imaginary thought-ropes consist of wrong attitudes and false viewpoints that do nothing for you.

Real thought-ropes consist of realistic ideas and truthful perceptions that change your life.

Do you really want to climb mountains? You now know how!

Mastering the Magic of Self-Science

The most valuable science in the world to you is self-science. With a firm grasp of who we are and what we can do, we become magicians capable of creating the kind of lives we really want. Without self-knowledge we have no central attachment; we are like loose spokes of a wheel without a hub.

Observes Dr. Lewis Mumford:

> *Only those who have achieved self-knowledge and are constantly seeking both to enlarge it and apply it in their daily living, are capable of overcoming their automatic reactions and reaching their own ideal limits.*[1]

---

[1] Lewis Mumford, *The Conduct of Life* (New York: Harcourt, Brace and World, Inc., 1951).

Think of self-science as a research project of enormous signifi-cance to you—for that is what it is.

I have found that many people respond to the challenge of self-understanding with two principal attitudes, at opposite poles to each other. One person replies, "Oh, but there's no need for self-study. I understand myself perfectly." Such people are usually in deep despair, well-masked beneath a gay exterior. But for any of us to really attain self-knowledge we must first honestly admit that we are strangers to ourselves. Epictetus, that wise Greek philosopher, pointed out long ago, "It is impossible for anyone to begin to learn what he thinks he already knows."

On the other extreme are those who throw up their arms and exclaim, "But I just can't find out what makes me tick. I've been trying for years." Such people need only apply the **Four Golden Keys** of Chapter 1 to a specific program of self-study. Their success is certain.

Psychology and psychiatry have done fine work in making clear the need for bringing subconscious negativities to the mind's surface where they can be handled. These sciences have made us aware of the lower levels of the mind where negativities hide out to do so much damage. But there is something else which is seen most clearly by the philosophers and religious teachers—like the New Testament writers, and in this day, Krishnamurti, George Gurdjieff, and P. D. Ouspensky. I speak of the *higher levels* of the mind. It is strange that we should be so hypnotized by the negative subconscious mind that we overlook the exalted superconsious mind! This lofty level of consciousness can be reached by anyone desiring it. You were created for such attainment.

There is no vague theory or misty mysticism in all this. We are discussing an entirely practical self-knowledge that can benefit you here and now. On this higher level of thinking a man has a courage and self-assurance of amazing quality.

As Alan G. discovered for himself:

Always Seek to Be Different

"My difficulty," he said during a discussion period, "is awkward self-expression. I get tongue-tied before people. I say dumb things. I don't speak smoothly and confidently. Maybe I blurt out a foolish remark before the boss; sometimes it's shyness with women.

You speak of these higher mental levels. How can they make me self-assured when speaking to other people?"

"Start by *not* trying to be conversationally clever. Have you noticed how you strain at saying the right thing?"

"Yes."

"Stop it. Right now. Don't try to be smooth. You see, Alan, as long as your mind dwells on this lower level of anxiety you will always speak awkwardly. Anxious words come from an anxious mind."

"Yes, I see that much. I think you are saying that I must work with my basic anxiety, not my conversations."

"Correct. But you can use your conversations to work on yourself. Don't rehearse your verbal scenes beforehand. Don't try to be clever. Act entirely differently; that is, *don't* try to make a good impression, and don't give a hoot if you make a poor one. If words arise spontaneously, speak; otherwise, remain silent. You must not be afraid of conversational silence. Incidentally, this is nine-tenths of social conversation—an embarrassed fear of silence."

Two or three members of the group smiled and nodded.

"What happens," asked Alan, "when I don't try to be clever?"

"By refusing to go along with your habitually anxious self, you loosen its grip on you. You have defied it. That starts an inner change that you can actually feel. And your personal confidence gradually rises to its naturally high level."

All of us noticed Alan's definite progress. For one thing, whenever he did speak up, people listened. A month or so after his original question, someone asked, "Please sum up this business of being at ease socially. How should we work on ourselves?"

"Don't try to be *better*; seek to be *different*."

Making the Most of Your Personal Power

At one time in ancient history, a man silently watched a river flow past his grassy camp. It occurred to him that he might sprawl atop a log and float down that river. By doing so, he used river-power for practical benefit. Later, another man wondered whether the afternoon breeze could be put to work. By building a wind-mill, he employed wind-power. Still later, man considered the possibility of harnessing the energy of the sun. Today, we have solar-power.

Stop and think. Look into your natural powers. Ask whether you are using them. Next, and of enormous importance to success, ask whether you are using them for *positive purpose*. It makes all the difference in your life. Your inner forces can be used either constructively or destructively. Let's look at a few of your inner energies:

Mental:

1. Imagination
2. Knowledge
3. Effort
4. Attention
5. Planning

Emotional:

1. Receptivity
2. Self-examination
3. Enthusiasm
4. Curiosity
5. Ambition

Physical:

1. Speech
2. Walking
3. Gestures
4. Lifting
5. Writing

Make an inquiry. Discover whether or not you use these personal powers for positive purposes.

Don't imagine fearful scenes. Use your imagination to create a bold program for success. Don't be receptive to all the negative ideas surrounding you. Receive only those that enrich and refresh. Don't speak in complaint. Speak with the assurance that the universe is on your side.

It really makes a great difference to you.

Ask Yourself Where You're Going Every Day

The value of any system of self-development should be tested by the actual enrichment it gives the individual using it.

A man has the right—no, the duty—to expect practical rewards from his selected system. In all fairness to himself he must inquire just how and where he is coming out a finer man than he was before. A chief barrier to a man's inner development is that he does not usually do this when desiring to change himself. Every man must frankly and courageously inquire of the plans he is using, "Are they *really* helping me to find myself? Are they *actually* working? In a very *practical* sense am I a bit freer and happier and more productive today than I was yesterday? Or, am I continuing with my present ideas merely because I have nowhere else to go?"

This can be quite a shocking question to ask yourself. It may reveal that you must change your plans. But this change could be the turning point in your life!

People are extremely practical when handling matters such as their finances or personal comfort. But, strangely, the larger the possible benefits the less a man inquires into practical possibilities. The reason for his timidity is his fear that if he asks for too much he will be too much disappointed.

Away with all that. A man must learn to defy his timidity and ask for the genuine product. If he persists, he will not be disappointed. The truths about life can never disappoint anyone. Only illusions cause dismay.

Man is much too timid. He must boldly ask for more. He must dare to strike out in favor of himself, *even while doubting the outcome*. The outcome is certain, but you will only know it by daring to strike out *before* you know it.

At one time, there was an undiscovered cavern in one of our Western states. A magnificent masterpiece of nature, its beauty was beyond imagination.

But no one came to see it. No one enjoyed its splendor. It was wasted.

Why? No one knew about it. Because it was undiscovered, it was unused. One day a roving cowboy chanced upon the opening. That was how New Mexico's Carlsbad Caverns became part of man's pleasure. [MENTAL PICTURE 41]

The point? We must dare to explore our natural resources. Undiscovered, we lose. We must tell ourselves about ourselves; then we hear the answer that sets us free.

How to Get the Greatest Encouragement of All

Let's take a practical for-instance. Let's suppose that your present system of thinking includes the idea that other people have power to hurt and upset you. If you think from this idea, you will certainly get hurt and upset. For one thing, your very expectancy draws them into the circle of your experience. But let's further suppose that you are so weary of getting hurt that you decide to think from a new idea, which is, *only the False Self can get hurt.* You reflect, "My True Self, which I am gradually discovering, cannot be hurt by anyone, anytime, anyplace." You have now done a really remarkable thing; namely, you have called the bluff of the False Self which gets so easily hurt. And you have begun to think from the new idea that the True Self is absolutely free of all hurt. Now, you are beginning to change inwardly. Now, even though someone makes an unkind remark, there is no longer a false idea in your mind which responds in hurt to it!

What has all this to do with self-confidence? *Everything*. By letting your True Self think for you, you are always confident. The True Self cannot be shaken by anything, not by loss of employment, by criticism, by being ignored, by anything whatsoever.

Dr. Rollo May explains it like this:

> *Our task, then, is to strengthen our consciousness of ourselves, to find centers of strength within ourselves which will enable us to stand despite the confusion and bewilderment around us.*[2]

One more thing. Nothing—absolutely nothing—is more encouraging than to actually see yourself becoming stronger and finding fresh resources. It is the greatest encouragement of all.

Do you see what a gigantic idea this really is?

Achieving Freedom from Frustration

Nothing drains a man's confidence more than repeated frustration. That is why people often ask, "Why are my attempts to reach my goals so often frustrated? How come my efforts don't win the prize?"

Let's find out.

---

[2] Rollo May, *Man's Search for Himself* (New York: W. W. Norton and Company, Inc., 1953).

To *do* something you must first *be* someone. Nothing is more impossible than to act above your own present level. The way to *do* more is to *be* more. This is somewhat difficult for us to grasp, but the man who works with this principle will find himself breaking through barriers that previously frustrated him.

We must change ourselves—the way we see things, the way we think and feel, our attitudes and viewpoints. As we elevate *ourselves*, we become perfectly equal to the *task* we have set for ourselves.

It is like a mountain climber who has scaled certain peaks but wants to go higher. To do this, he must alter his thinking toward *himself*, not toward the higher peak. He must strengthen his muscles for the longer climb, he must gather additional supplies, he might need special equipment, and so on. If he attempts to climb to a higher peak while using lower-peak equipment, he makes defeat and frustration necessary. [MENTAL PICTURE 42]

We must not miss this vital principle. It is too easy to blame the peak instead of examining our peak-scaling capacities.

Higher peaks of achievement await every man or woman, and frustration in reaching them is completely unnecessary. Go to work on yourself. The moment your *being* goes higher, your *doing* rises right along with it.

Someone requested, "Will you please give us one good plan for elevating ourselves?"

"Stop looking for ways to do things and simply start doing them."

Start Using the Strangely Neglected Power

We now come to a personal power that is strangely neglected by millions of people. We have met it briefly in previous pages, but now is the time for a complete exploration. It could well be the exact force you need for changing everything.

The reason for its neglect is probably that very few people have ever understood it. But now you can load up with its power and fire toward your personal targets.

Let's call it the Power of Discard.

You speed confidently forward not by *acquiring* something,

but by first *discarding* something. It's like a ship that revives its inner power by discarding a useless, burdensome cargo.

Man is like a ship. Though naturally powerful, he founders at sea because of unnecessary mental cargoes. As he drops them through fresh insight, he sails steadily toward his ports.

The immense truth is:

Our growth into full personal power is basically a process of discard.

Discard *what?*

> *Unrealistic beliefs*
> *Unworkable assumptions*
> *Painful imaginations*
> *False conclusions*
> *Impulsive decisions*
> *Hazy judgments*

Do you see the connection between this and what we have previously covered? A main lesson is this: We find the True Self —with all its natural power, by abandoning the False Self—with all its weakness and confusion.

When you discard unworkable assumptions, *something happens;* something that is really quite amazing. Here is how Dr. Fritz Kunkel describes the startling change:

> *Now another avenue is open towards this goal. It comes from inside themselves, not with moral commands but with creative power. It is really their better Self . . . The most amazing thing is that this new and unheard-of power is at the same time well-known and familiar to them. They have felt, thought, dreamt all this many times. Only they were never able to express it clearly enough . . . And then the most unexpected thing happens: a new clarity and certainty, and a new and deeper consciousness are there; the real Self and its creative forces begin the new work . . . it proves that there is a way . . .* [8]

Discovering Your Superior Self

All this is great news. As we rid our minds of the false, we make room for the true, just as a cleared field can grow flowers. As we have seen, you already possess all the mental force you

---

[8] Fritz Kunkel, *In Search of Maturity* (New York: Charles Scribner's Sons, 1943).

need for confident conquest; that force needs only to be loosened, to be free to work. Take, for instance, the state of *courage*. Courage isn't the opposite of fear; it's the absence of fear. By ridding our minds of fear, our courage rises naturally, effortlessly—just as the morning sun, no longer blocked by the mountain, appears brightly before us.

As a young man just out of high school, I went to work in a grocery market. One day, the manager asked me to do some minor bookkeeping. Since arithmetic had never been a strong subject for me I told him I hadn't the ability to do the work. He said quietly, "Vernon, I didn't ask whether you had the ability. Just go ahead, please, and do it."

Well, I did it. In those few words (far kindlier than I realized at the time) he helped rid my mind of its false belief in inability. As that false notion fled, confidence arrived.

A man is courageous and confident to the degree that he distinguishes between truth and falsehood about himself. The truth is, he is vastly superior to what he imagines himself to be. But because he fails to see this truth, because he carelessly ignores it, he fails to experience the wonderful new life that could be his. As he grows in mental perception, he sees that the truth about himself is what he *really* wanted all along. He really didn't want to be angry; he just wanted to preserve his self-esteem. He really didn't want his neighbor's wife; he only wanted assurance of his attractiveness. As a man opens himself to psychological truth, falsehood falls away. Then, he is free from the agonizing need to prove himself day after day.

Work with your Power of Discard. Abandon all mental motions that don't provide genuine satisfaction. Then, you will find your confident self, just as the sculptor finally comes to the fine figure within the block.

Handling the Unexpected

As we have seen, the power of a Mental Picture lies in its ability to slip past negative thoughts and take root in the mind. Here it does its purifying work. It starts by changing the way you see things, including those daily difficulties around the home or office. You begin to see people in an entirely different light, a light that keeps you emotionally peaceful, even when other people are unkind or troublesome. You may exclaim, as do others who have this light, "How could I have ever lived in that old, unhappy way? What a fantastic difference!"

I want to show you how one Mental Picture changed everything for Walter C. This story will increase your excitement over the benefits of Psycho-Pictography.

Walter, a salesman, had clarified his problem, so he came right to the point:

"Unexpected events bother me. I find it hard to handle sudden changes in a routine. It's especially annoying in my saleswork. For instance, I plan my calls on a certain schedule, then, a client phones to say he can't make it. As hard as I try not to let it bother me, it still does. How can I be more at ease in adjusting to sudden switches?"

In order to form a Mental Picture in his mind, I told the following story:

A man was invited to a party. Misunderstanding the invitation, he thought it was a costume party, so he dressed up as a Confederate colonel. Upon arriving, he discovered that it wasn't a costume party after all; everyone was in everyday dress. Of course, he was annoyed and embarrassed. So he went home, changed to normal clothes, and went back to enjoy the party. [MENTAL PICTURE 43]

The point is this: don't dress up in the wrong mental clothing. By doing this, you find yourself out of harmony with the realities of the situation. Be totally flexible. Don't demand that your preconceived ideas be confirmed by the eventual reality of the situation. Simply let the situation be whatever it wants to be. This flexibility keeps you at peace *regardless* of what happens. Experiment with this. You will discover that a cheerfully flexible mind is a comfortable mind.

Using Your New Language Effectively

Norma L. commented, "I really try to understand what you say, but I just can't grasp the meaning. I have a flickering feeling that there is something of extraordinary importance here, but it's all so vague. I'm intensely interested in understanding these truths but haven't the key. Do you see my problem?"

"Yes, perfectly. Don't worry about it. Your confusion is quite natural. I assure you the light will dawn. Let me give you an illustration:

Suppose you go to a lecture to hear a speaker whom you believe has a valuable message. You settle yourself comfortably with every intention of listening and understanding. The lecturer speaks. To your surprise, you don't understand a word he says. As hard as you try, you just can't absorb meaning from his words. The whole thing is a mystery. Finally, you discover that the lecturer was speaking in Swedish, a language you don't understand.

This makes you feel much better, for you see that it isn't stupidity on your part after all. No, you just don't understand that particular language.

Now you see what you must do: in order to understand, you must learn to listen in this other language. So you study Swedish for a couple of weeks, then go once again to hear that lecturer. *Now* you understand him, at least a bit. You continue to study Swedish, and, each time, that lecturer makes more sense to you. Finally, when you yourself learn to speak that new language, you also understand when another speaks it.

This is your present problem, Norma. You are being addressed in a new psychological language but are listening in another. You see, a lower level of understanding cannot grasp the higher. [MENTAL PICTURE 44]

Let me add one thing: Some people scoff at these ideas of self-development. They think them boring or nonsensical. If they don't speak this higher psychological language, these ideas *always* appear nonsensical. If a man takes *his* language as the *only* language, he will scoff when you tell him of another language, one entirely new and superior. In a very real way, this is a language from another psychological world.

Psycho-Pictography has been carefully prepared to teach you the language of a higher mind. This wonderful new language contains no words meaning *anxiety, loneliness, despair.*

PLANS FOR MORE SELF-CONFIDENCE

1. Learn to think from practical and profitable ideas. They increase self-trust.
2. Practice the magic of self-science. Self-knowledge never fails to enrich you.
3. Don't try to be *better;* seek to be *different.*
4. Search out and employ your personal powers.
5. Strike out in favor of yourself. Have no concern over results of your bold adventure.
6. Your True Self is fully confident in every situation.
7. Alter your thinking toward yourself. You have more natural strength than you realize.
8. Remember the enormous Power of Discard. This is a major secret for finding lasting power.
9. Learn to be mentally flexible in every situation.
10. Psycho-Pictography teaches you a new way of living in which there is no timidity—only courage.

How to Live Every Day to Its Fullest Measure

Life is worth living when you understand its rich worth.

This understanding is the purpose of this chapter.

Let's start with the question, *Where are you living? What mental world do you inhabit?* It is important to find out.

A story from ancient Egypt tells of a young prince who lived with his father, the Pharaoh, in a palace along the banks of the River Nile. Restless, as young men are, the prince set out one morning in search of adventure. The Pharaoh warned, "Stay near the safety and refreshment of the river. Don't wander into the dry desert."

The prince heeded the advice for a while. But curiosity and carelessness led him away from the Nile and into the desert. He soon lost his sense of direction. Confusion and anxiety set in. The pangs of thirst and the dangers of wild beasts made every step a torment. The Pharaoh, watching from afar, saw his son's despair, but could not help. Under Egyptian law, anyone who willingly wandered into the desert had to find his own way back. There was a way out, but every wanderer had to see it for himself.

Sensing that his suffering was needless, and that there was a way out, the prince went to work. By persistently eliminating each false direction in turn, he finally found his way back to the palace. [MENTAL PICTURE 45]

That story applies to the physical world, but has a perfect parallel in your mental world.

Where are you living mentally? In the dryness of confusion and tiredness? It is really unnecessary. Think back to a time, perhaps a few years ago, when you were *free*. Catch a glimpse of the refreshing days you used to have. *There* is where you can live once more.

No wide-awake man wanders unnecessarily in a real desert. He walks out. But people do not see that they unnecessarily waste themselves by remaining in a mental wilderness. They fail to understand their rightful refreshment found in a mental palace. They mistakenly take esoteric parables as pleasant little lessons, but do not see them as life-liberating truths. We must wake up!

In which mental world are you living? It is really quite easy to tell. If you live every day with inner ease and luxury, you occupy a mental palace. If not, then you have a bright experience just ahead. You can travel to such a luxurious life. For the next few weeks, use the Guides at the front of this book. Each of them is a road home.

Who Is Living Your Life?

The following dialogue took place during a discussion. I asked someone:

"Who is living your life for you?"

"Why, no one. I live my own life."

"What causes you to live the kind of life you live; what makes you do what you do?"

"My attitudes and viewpoints and convictions. Obviously, the way we think determines the way we act."

"And where did you get these attitudes? How come you think

the way you do? Where did you get your viewpoints toward sex, politics, religion, people, and everything else?"

"Oh, I picked them up from other people in my early years."

"Then they are not a part of your original self; they are merely *acquired*?"

"Yes, that must be so."

"Then you are living according to the attitudes and viewpoints of other people who passed them on to you?"

"Well, yes."

"Then you are not really living your own life?"

"I see what you mean. I am repeating what others told me. In a sense, I am living *their* life."

"What if many of these acquired attitudes are wrong, unrealistic, damaging? For instance, suppose you believe that it's impossible to switch from anxiety to happiness?"

"Then I pay the price for that false belief."

"Do you like paying the price?"

"Not at all."

"Must you continue to suffer from false viewpoints?"

"No."

"Why not?"

"Because I can drop them. Since they are merely acquired, like uncomfortable clothing, I can shed them like clothing."

"Then?"

"Then, for the first time, I'll live my own life."

"You like that idea?"

"I'm ready!"

How to Return to Yourself

What a dawning appears to the man or woman who earnestly inquires, "Who is living my life for me? Am I really thinking for myself or am I unknowingly projecting acquired ideas which may be all wrong?"

Such a sincere person begins to see that he is *not* his acquired viewpoints, *not* his adopted beliefs, *not* his habitual reactions. He begins to separate the true from the false. He divides the assumed self from the real self. He sees that he is not all these thought-clothes. So he takes them off.

You are not your thought-clothes any more than you are the gray suit or blue dress you wear.

As we discard our conditioned ideas about ourselves, we discover who we really are. And when you know who you really are, a miracle happens. Suffering and sorrow and conflict go away forever. And I assure you that these are not mere words; they are living truths that you can experience for yourself.

You sometimes see a television drama unfold like this:

A spy is assigned to penetrate enemy territory. He is given a new name and supplied with a set of false identifications. He is taught to speak and act and think in a way foreign to his real nature. He is trained to imitate the manners and customs of the enemy land. In short, he assumes a false identity.

He spends the next two or three years in the foreign land, acting out his role. The unnatural manners and customs become habitual.

His assignment ends. The spy returns to his home country. Trouble begins. His false role comes into conflict with his original life. He is awkward and confused. He can't separate his false self from his original self. *He doesn't know who he is.*

But he is courageous and wise. Seeing the problem, he goes to work on himself. He gradually drops his acquired acts and thoughts. He returns to his true identity. All is well once more. He lives in peace. [MENTAL PICTURE 46]

That is what happens to people. Having unconsciously taken on foreign identifications, they no longer know who they really are. So enters conflict and pain.

But, like that spy, we can be wise. We can gradually drop all false ideas and identifications. *We can return to ourselves.*

It is perfectly possible for you to discover who you really are. What a delightful surprise!

Sometimes in our meetings we have advanced discussions. We plunge into deeper psychological waters where the more precious pearls are found. One such dive sprang from the remark, "I know I'm imprisoned, but haven't the slightest idea who my jailor is."

"If you only knew how free you are!"

"Really? I'm actually at inner liberty right now?"

"Yes, but you don't see this as yet. You are your own unconscious jailor. Your problems and griefs and conflicts are of your own making."

"Why don't I see this as yet?"

"Because your False Self lives in dread of its dethronement. Whenever it suspects that you are looking for a way out, it gets terrified. And it fights! This, try to see, is why you get *extra* scared the moment you determine to break free. Sensing a threat to its existence, the False Self fires its full arsenal of weapons at you."

"What are its weapons?"

"For one thing, the False Self tries to make you feel guilty and disloyal at the thought of abandoning it. Also, it makes full use of man's mental laziness. It slyly whispers the greatest lie of all—that no state really exists other than its own miserable one. This is its chief weapon of terror—to hint that your plunge away from the False Self is a plunge toward a terrifying nothingness. But the truth is, this new nothingness turns out to be a world of fantastic light and freedom."

"While the False Self is causing all this commotion, what is the True Self doing?"

"Gently trying to get you to listen to the truth that you are free and always have been. It urges you to see that you are not a slave to the illusions whispered by the False Self. It tells you that the False Self is bluffing, and that you have power to call that bluff. Remember, the True Self is the voice of Truth."

"This is the most thrilling idea I have ever heard in my life!"

"If you only knew how free you are!"

How to Learn the Secrets of Living Magic

The entire purpose of Mental Pictures is a *change in self*. This comes before all else. Your basic plan is to change the way you think, speak, act, feel, respond, and perceive. In other words, we are after *living magic*.

Attempts to change exterior conditions without first altering the inner self are a sad waste of energy. A person can go ahead and switch his residence or profession or friends, but, unless self-change comes first, he will not find lasting satisfaction in them.

As *we* change, our *world* changes. The author of *The Conquest of Illusion* explains it like this:

> When we have seen the vision of Reality our world is changed, utterly and almost beyond recognition, and yet nothing has changed in things as they are, it is but that we have gained a new vision . . . It is the new vision, which is born when man is freed from the tyranny of illusion, that the whole world is changed and appears radiant with love and beauty, apparently utterly changed, though the change really is in man himself alone.[1]

Suppose you enter a dark room and flip the light switch, but nothing happens. The room remain dark. You find that the light bulb is at fault. Now, you wouldn't keep flipping the switch in hopes that the bulb would somehow come to life. No, you wouldn't do that. You would realize that *that* bulb has no capacity for illumination. So you wisely decide that a change is needed. You set aside the useless bulb and replace it with an entirely new and lively one. You now have a different kind of bulb, one capable of giving you an entirely new look at that room. Now, you see things clearly, you can walk safely and enjoyably around the room. It becomes comfortable at last. [MENTAL PICTURE 47]

Likewise, a change in the inner self illuminates everything on the outside. Our day becomes living magic.

How to Banish Boredom

What about the problem of boredom? We clearly see it to be a painful state; one that drains life of its richness. What can be done?

The story is told of the man who sat at a piano and tapped endlessly upon a single key. Day after day he sat down at the piano to strike that one key only. It bored him to tears.

Whenever his family asked him why he played the same boring key, he replied, "I don't know why I do it. I just do it." Whenever his neighbors complained of the monotonous note he answered, "I'm sorry, but that's the way it is. I wish someone would tell me how to strike another note."

---

[1] J. J. Van Der Leeuw, *The Conquest of Illusion* (New York: Alfred A. Knopf, Incorporated, 1951).

A famous teacher of the piano was finally called in. He examined the problem, then announced, "The reason you play that single note is because you don't see that there are many other notes to play. In short, you are hypnotized by that single note."

The man replied, "But that's silly. I can see every one of those other notes. There are eighty-seven of them. I see them plainly enough."

"No," the teacher explained, "if you really saw those notes you would try to play them. Everyone wants to play more than one note. When they don't, it's because they don't really see them. You think that that one note is all there is. You are hypnotized by it."

"Really?" asked the bewildered man.

"Really. You see, you are bored because you play that one note only. You play that one note only because you think that no other notes exist. You must come out of your hypnosis. You must see the other notes. You must experiment with them. And you must not be afraid of the strange sound you hear at first. As you play, they will become more and more familiar and less and less frightening. Then, that familiarity will turn to harmony. And then you will never be bored again. You will have the entire keyboard to play upon."

Boredom indicates lack of insight into the vast expanse of life. We hypnotically play the single note we see, perhaps that of worry or depression, not realizing that such single notes can produce no harmony. Our primary aim must be to become inwardly free individuals. With that as our healthy aim, we learn the new notes that give us variety and harmony.

The person with an enthusiasm for the truth *about* life need never worry about his enthusiasm *for* life.

How to Have Freedom from the Negative Self

Deep down inside, every man suspects that he really has only one problem. He somehow realizes, however dimly, that his problems are caused by his negative self. Even when he pretends to others that all is well, he knows he is not kidding *himself*.

But this suspicion that something is wrong can be the means for making things right. An admission that we are on the wrong track enables us to switch directions. The truth is within every man; it bursts through and destroys the negative self upon our honest invitation. Then, life is lived in full measure.

Henry David Thoreau's testimony is ample evidence that the full life can be found:

> *I learned this, at least, by my experiment: that if one advances confidently in the direction of his dreams, and endeavors to live the life which he has imagined, he will meet with a success unexpected in common hours. He will put some things behind, will pass an invisible boundary; new, universal, and more liberal laws will begin to establish themselves around and within him . . . and he will live with the license of a higher order of beings. In proportion as he simplifies his life, the laws of the universe will appear less complex, and solitude will not be solitude, nor poverty poverty, nor weakness weakness. If you have built castles in the air, your work need not be lost; that is where they should be. Now put the foundations under them.*

One phrase fascinates me: "In proportion as he simplifies his life, the laws of the universe will appear less complex . . ." Let's investigate.

A man living in a large city is beset by a multitude of laws and regulations and statutes. Wherever he turns he finds a traffic law or a building code or a merchandising prohibition in his way. His liberty to do this or that is restricted.

Suppose that man moves to the countryside, to the simpler life. Because he is no longer under the laws of the big city, he moves about with much greater liberty. [MENTAL PICTURE 48]

That is what happens to the man who removes himself from his own negative self. Because he moves away from his negative emotions and false ideas, he lives in liberty.

The nice part of it all is that this is something any man can really do for himself.

The Greatest Inspiration on Earth

A college professor asked his students, "What, in your opinion, is the greatest inspiration on earth?" The replies came:

"A pink sunset."

"A sublime thought."

"A happy person."

"A colorful garden."

The professor said, "Yes, all of those are certainly inspiring. Let me give you my reply to that question. The greatest inspiration on earth is something that really works."

The professor explained, "My idea of inspiration is *whatever adds practical value to mankind*. It includes the ideas you supplied. An inspiration is something that actually, in a very real way, makes people happier and healthier."

Stop and consider that idea for a moment. It is both strange and attractive: The greatest inspiration on earth is something *practical*. We usually don't associate inspiration with practical matters of life, but we should.

I call this to your attention for an interesting reason. In reading these pages, some may inquire, "The ideas inspire me, but are they practical? Will they make my daily life easier and happier? Can they help me in making decisions, lowering mental pressures, in doing things the easy way?"

The answer?

There is nothing more practical than the truth-that-inspires. In classwork, we prove it by dialogues like these:

"What conquers nervousness?"

"The truth about our rightful calm."

"Then what is more practical than the truth?"

"What cures heartache?"

"The finding of the True Self."

"Then what is more useful than finding yourself?"

The greatest inspiration on earth is the truth. That is because nothing works like the truth. People should try it. Nothing is more practical. What is more practical than being happy?

Take a New Look at Attitudes

"You have stated many times," said a woman in our group, "that stuffy living is caused by our wrong attitudes. I can grasp this is in a way, yet, why do I continue with these self-destructive attitudes?"

"Because you don't really see that they are working against you. In one way or another, you are justifying them. How difficult—and yet how enriching—it is for someone to really see what he is doing to himself!"

"Why is it so hard for me to change my attitudes?"

"Because you identify with them. You think that you *are* your attitudes. You think that your abandonment of these attitudes will leave you empty, a nobody, without support. But this is exactly what you must dare to do. You must drop your false mental viewpoints without immediately substituting others. At first, this emptiness will leave you somewhat disturbed, puzzled. But stick with the vacancy, dare to face the emptiness. Then it will be filled with truth, just as a lake with brackish water must be drained before being refilled with fresh water."

"Dare to be without a harmful attitude, such as resentment or self-pity? Is that the idea? Can we experiment in our daily lives with this?"

"Yes, and with fine results. Select, for example, some negative attitude or feeling you have toward another person. Dare to be without it. Have the courage to drop it entirely. In time, the light will dawn. That negative feeling will vanish completely. You will never again he bothered by your own attitude toward that person. You are chained to anyone you dislike. Have you ever noticed that? Watch it. See that you are the slave of anyone toward whom you have a negative feeling. But drop the attitude and the other person vanishes from your emotional life. So does your pain vanish."

"Can this technique be applied to other situations, such as depression?"

"Of course. It is your attitude toward a situation that causes depression, not the situation. You may not believe this as yet, but experiment with it and you will see. All depression is totally unnecessary."

How to Love

What about the positive virtues, like love, patience, humility, that make for a rich life? How can we acquire them?

They appear spontaneously when you find yourself. The True Self possesses all these natural virtues. But there is something of extreme importance for you to remember. Every genuine virtue has its counterfeit.

The counterfeit of humility could be an assumed pose for the purpose of making a good impression. Someone may want something from you, and so he presents a pleasant and kindly manner. But it will vanish quickly enough if he is thwarted. His real nature then reveals itself, perhaps in rage or arrogance. You must be very careful that you do not assume that other people are what they appear to be. You must be a wise judge of human nature.

A positive virtue—the real thing—is not something that you *do*. It is something that you *are*. A genuinely kindly man and his kindness are a single unit; they are *one*. A really gentle person cannot help acting with kindness any more than a cruel person can help but act with cruelty.

Do not be afraid to face the existence of negative attitudes and emotions within you. Simply see that they are there. Remember, they are not the real you; they are acquired negativities. Once you really see this you will go to work on yourself in a new way.

How to Have a Mental Magic Party

I want to supply you with some profitable facts about a Mental Magic Party. Tested plans for holding a Mental Magic Party are supplied in my previous book, *SECRETS OF MENTAL MAGIC: How to Use Your Full Power of Mind.*

Briefly defined, a Mental Magic Party is a gathering of men and women who earnestly want to change their lives. This change can mean many things, including freedom from negative emotions, finding a genuine purpose in life, and discovering practical answers to everyday problems.

Definite progress is achieved by those in attendance. A businessman sees that he is quite capable of handling a complex financial problem with inner tranquility. A homemaker finds a new way to clear up a crisis with the children. A married couple discovers that a change in attitude turns into a miracle of niceness in their relationship. Difficulties relating to sex are understood and dissolved.

Progress comes through understanding the same ideas we are covering in this book. Self-knowledge plays its vital role. So does the capacity to listen with a receptive mind. Those attending a Mental Magic Party learn practical rules for their human relations. Scoring advances is something like an army battling along a ten mile front. It attacks first here, then there, scoring a small victory in this area, and a smashing triumph at another point. And so it goes, with the entire front moving ahead steadily. [MENTAL PICTURE 49]

The question-and-answer periods of a Mental Magic Party always provide some helpful ideas. Examples:

"What has the inner life of a man to do with outer affairs; for instance, how can we have better government?"

"The final answer to better government is not in more laws or changed laws but in the personal integrity and maturity in the characters of both our lawmakers and those who vote them into office."

"Is it wrong to try to get things from other people?"

"It is not wrong to want something from someone else as long as your desire does him no harm."

"In spite of all my studies and activities I am not really any better off than I was before. What can I do?"

"Moving from one corner to another in a stalled elevator does not carry you upward. Make sure you are using the genuine principles of progress, such as self-honesty and sincere intention. Upward movement can be *felt;* there is no mistaking it."

Picture an Oasis

At our meetings, we follow the course of action urged in this book, that is, the use of illustrations and examples, called Mental Pictures. One evening, someone spoke up, "You once said that in the psychological world the rich get richer and the poor get poorer. I know that this is taught in the New Testament, but why is it so? How come a man with a fair amount of insight tends to get more, while the person who has very little tends to lose even that which he has?"

Because life is not static. You either grow or you regress. The choice is yours. Here is a Mental Picture to make it clearer:

Picture a green oasis in the middle of the desert, rich with cool water and refreshing shade. It offers a peaceful and healthy life.

A mile away, out in the hot desert, a man is lost. But he is close enough to the oasis to catch a glimpse of it. He can see the difference between the greenery of the oasis and the gray sands around him. *Because he can see merely that much, he is encouraged to find more.* And so he heads for the oasis, growing closer, richer, with each step.

But take another wanderer, three miles distant from the oasis. Because he is farther away he is less likely to look and be encouraged. So he turns in the wrong direction and wanders even farther and farther away. Because he can see nothing of the oasis he wanders in despair and bitterness. In that state he is likely to see an illusionary oasis, a mirage. And so his life is wasted in stumbling toward one illusion after another.

The point is this: The closer we come to the Truth the more we value it. Then, because we value it more, we come even closer. That is why the rich get richer. They earn it with their own effort

Any wanderer can change direction at anytime. No one needs to be lost. Any man or woman, through right action, can find the oasis. [MENTAL PICTURE 50]

You, the reader, can form your own study group by using plans provided in Chapter 15. You can call it a Mental Magic Party or Psycho-Pictography Study Group, depending upon which book you use as textbook. The object is to meet with other men and women who suspect the existence of an oasis and who want to search together.

The beauty of it all is that the oasis really exists.

FOR YOUR RICHER DAY

1. Life is worth living when you understand the rich worth of life.
2. Walk out of the mental desert.
3. Live your own life. It belongs to you.
4. You find your genuine self as you discard all acquired attitudes about yourself. Discard them.

5. *If you only knew how free you are!*

6. Boredom disappears forever as you catch an insight into the vast expanse of life. You can catch this insight.

7. Life becomes richer and more meaningful as you find liberty from the negative self.

8. The greatest inspiration on earth is something practical, something that really works. Therefore, the truth is utterly practical.

9. The positive emotions of love and affection and patience appear when you find your True Self.

10. Plan a Psycho-Pictography Study Group. Tested plans are supplied in Chapter 15.

9

How You Can Expel
Emotional Troubles Quickly

Have you ever considered *attention* as a personal power for your benefit? It is just that. By attention I mean the simple act of directing your mind toward something specific. A distressed person is someone who has not learned to attend to distress-dissolving ideas. He gets distracted by negative emotions or wanders off into profitless desires.

Picture a man lost at sea in a small boat. He is blocked off by thick fog. But he remembers something that he saw before the fog set in. He recalls a cottage set high on the cliffs of shore. So he turns his attention and his boat in that direction. Every so often the fog drifts apart just long enough for him to catch a brief glimpse of the cottage. But that is enough. He realizes that his attention to that cottage is all that is necessary. By attending rightly, he cannot fail. And so he succeeds in cutting through the fog and reaching shore. [MENTAL PICTURE 51]

Experiment with the power of attention. Select a basic principle from these pages. Give it your wholehearted attention and interest. Reflect on it as you go through your day. Try to see its value to you.

Take, for instance, the idea we covered in Chapter 5: *We are most helpful to other people when we first have our own lives pretty well in hand.* When something goes wrong with your automobile, you don't think about your neighbor's car. You examine and correct your own. Then, should your neighbor have trouble with his car, you have the knowledge and skill for genuine help. Personal value comes first. Then we have lasting value for others.

This idea might help you to see that it is not selfish to think about your personal development. That alone is great advancement for many people, especially those bothered by a false sense of guilt.

Remember, no effort at attending to the right things is lost. It always pays a profit.

Scientist Sir Isaac Newton declared, "If I have ever made any valuable discoveries, it has been owing more to patient attention, than to any other talent."

Let your attention give you valuable discoveries.

How to Increase Your Inner Peace

I want to give you a tested technique for gradually and surely increasing your inner peace. It works for you regardless of the noise and confusion that may surround your day.

You will detach yourself as a mental participant in these noisy events. You will observe them, be aware of them, but will not involve yourself mentally or emotionally. Perhaps you ask, "But can this really be done? It sounds impossible to separate myself from the constant clatter around me." I assure you that it can be done by you.

You see, your True Self *is* detached from everything on the outside. It has *awareness* of exterior conditions but does not get emotionally upset by them. You have a True Self at this very moment. At the very instant of reading these lines you are capable of mental detachment from all exterior problems.

Be a calm beholder of life. Mentally detach yourself. Stand back and quietly observe everything that happens to you and around you. Do not resist it; merely observe. Do not try to change or improve or destroy it, merely be aware. See yourself as someone apart, which, in truth, you are.

You need not fear that this detachment loses your control of things. It does not harm your daily tasks. They will go on as before. It may surprise you to find them proceeding as before, even improved. Mental detachment is, in fact, a higher form of control.

Picture yourself looking out the tower of your walled castle. You observe everything going on below you in the outside world. Some men are fighting in open combat. Others are slyly deceiving their neighbors with smooth words and empty promises. You observe the whole miserable mess, but are not a participant. If foolish men want to fight each other, let them do so, but you will have nothing to do with the madness. You will not sacrifice your life to their folly. [MENTAL PICTURE 52]

This kind of detachment is not retreat from reality; it is a healthy *perception* of it.

Stand apart and behold your life. It detaches you from trouble. *You* don't suffer from *that* ill-tempered man; *you* don't get depressed over *that* tragic event; *you* don't pay the price for *that* form of mankind's madness. *You are free.*

How to Prevent Your Emotions from Alienating People

When we carefully examine our negative emotions we always find them directed against some other person. Even when we seem to resent our circumstances we secretly or openly blame others for those circumstances. So it is important that we clarify our feelings as they relate to other people. It clears everything in a surprising way.

It is strange how human beings miss the most obvious facts about their negativities toward others. A hateful man seldom reasons, "Hatred toward others makes me miserable, so in the name of common sense I'd better abandon it." Rarely does a resentful person think, "Resentment of other people drains my strength and destroys my mental powers, so I'd better clear it from my life." Negative feelings so cloud a man with darkness that he cannot see what he is doing to himself.

Sooner or later, all of us must see that negative feelings toward another person is like tossing dust at him while the wind blows against us. It all comes back. This is not merely a moralistic teaching or Sunday school lesson; it is a basic and inescapable Law of Life.

Commented Paul B., "I know you are right, but you arouse contradiction in me. I want to grasp these ideas, but I also resist them. What is all this?"

"It is a good sign. It means that you are challenging your false notions—and they don't like it. Remember, all inner contradiction is between the truth which is in you and falsehood. Keep challenging your false ideas. As they disappear, conflict ceases. Then you are at peace with the truth."

Added Barbara L., "But what about people who do not challenge their false assumptions? Are they peaceful? Are they without this inner battle?"

"No. Their conflict is merely covered up. Most people are subconsciously miserable."

Don't be afraid of the added anxiety that arises whenever you challenge a false notion. It is temporary, just as you must temporarily battle the waves in order to arrive at the calm sea beyond the shore. You see, once you challenge your negative feelings they fight back, so your pressure increases for a while.

Most people run for cover whenever a negative feeling is exposed to the light of consciousness, consequently, they remain in darkness. You can be a hero. Dare to stand in the light. After a while, you will see that the very light you once feared is the very light of your life.

How the Adventures of Don Quixote Apply to You

Do you remember the fascinating and somewhat pathetic Don Quixote, hero of the Spanish novel by Miguel de Cervantes? A pleasant and harmless gentleman, Don Quixote had read too many stories about dashing knights in armor. He imagined himself to be one of them. Dressing himself in rusty armor and mounting a creaky horse, he set forth to find adventure and romance.

Poor Don Quixote! One time he attacked a windmill, thinking it was a swinging giant. Another time he charged into a flock of sheep, imagining it to be an enemy army. He was as sincere as his mental mix-up permitted, but so utterly wrong. He just couldn't see things as they really were. Worst of all, he didn't know who he really was. [MENTAL PICTURE 53]

Many men and women are in the same unhappy position. Though eager to venture forth to conquer the world, everything goes wrong. They fail to see the cause. It is not the world that is wrong; it is our vision of it. And when our vision is faulty, so are our emotions. We become frightened of other people because we mistakenly think they have power to hurt us. They haven't. We angrily attack a social condition, perhaps loss of employment, because we feel insecure. What we don't see is that the insecurity is based on ego-damage, not in the employment, which we can, with some energy, always solve. We fear the silence and so chatter endlessly, or chase madly around, hoping to drown out the terror of the silence. We fail to see that fear of silence is solved by facing it, welcoming it, and finally embracing it.

Don Quixote didn't know who he was. In his fear of his nothingness he set up imaginary pictures of who he was. In his imagination he was a dashing knight and great lover and bold adventurer. But when those imaginary pictures clashed with reality, he toppled from his horse.

"But," someone asked, "how can I discover who I really am?"

Do not try to discover who you really are. Find out who you are *not*. You are not your imaginary pictures of yourself. Once you see who you are *not*, you will know who you *are*. It is something far different than you now think. It is miraculous. You will feel entirely different toward yourself and everything else. In other words, you will feel good.

How to Change Feelings That Are Holding You Back

Perhaps you say, "I agree that our mental attitudes decide the way we feel, but how can I experiment with this in a practical way? How can I take a specific situation and feel better toward it?"

You are right. The way you think toward a situation has everything to do with the way you feel toward it. Change the thinking, and you alter the feeling. Many people agree with this intellectually, but we must do more than that. We must experiment personally until we really see how true it is.

I will give you an experiment that will show you how. You can perform it at once. You will then see in a very real way that a change in thought creates a change in feeling.

Here it is:

Take some specific situation that bothers you. It can be anything at all, but let's select *loneliness* for our experiment. Suppose you are troubled by the feeling that you are left out of life, excluded from activity with other people, no one is interested enough to write or phone you. Now, you don't like this feeling of isolation. It is painful and somewhat frightening. You want to escape it. So this is your present emotional feeling toward loneliness—you don't like it.

Your attitude of not liking this situation creates that uncomfortable feeling. In other words, the way you *think* toward it creates a corresponding feeling. So here you are, trapped inside a cage of your own thoughts and feelings.

So we come to the big question: How can we feel at peace with this thought of being alone?

We reverse our attitude toward the situation. We tell ourselves that we *like* being alone, we actually *enjoy* our solitude. This is what we *want*. We *like* what we previously disliked. *And we no longer mistake aloneness for loneliness.*

Never doubt but that your troublesome feelings will fight you at first. They are habitual tenants who don't like the idea of eviction. Expect this resistance and don't give in. Just continue to enjoy your situation. The negative feelings will grow weaker and weaker.

You can use this marvelous technique in any bothersome circumstance. Go against the current. Like what you don't like. Miracles happen!

Now You Can Enjoy Yourself Every Day

People are often puzzled by the idea of making life more enjoyable by changing their viewpoints. Let's examine it.

Suppose you are not feeling well one day, yet you accompany some friends on a leisurely drive through the beautiful countryside. Someone calls your attention to a lovely lake, but because of your illness, you cannot give it your attention or interest. Someone else remarks about a magnificent mountain in the distance, but you hardly hear him. You pass one lovely scene after another, yet they have no meaning to you. Because your illness has taken all your energy, you have none to spare in enjoying yourself. It is the same to your mind as if these natural beauties didn't exist at all. In your present ill state, they have neither existence nor attraction.

But the next day you recover. You feel fine. There is no inward attention to anything; you are outward bound once more. So again you go on a drive; you visit the very same places. But now, everything is completely different. You enjoy the lovely lake and magnificent mountain. You respond to them. You enjoy yourself.

How come? It was the very same scenery both times. But on the second trip *you* were different. You saw everything in an entirely new way. You had the inner freedom to see and appreciate your outer world. Like magic, your changed mental viewpoint changed the world for you. [MENTAL PICTURE 54]

It is difficult for people to grasp that the very same principle holds true elsewhere in life. Yet it is absolutely so. When we are inwardly ill at ease we do not really see things as *they* are; we see them as *we* are. And there is a world of difference—an actual world of difference—in the two viewpoints.

As we elevate our mental viewpoints we also elevate our world. How is this accomplished? Let's return again to a basic principle of this book: enjoyment results from discard, not from acquisition. Discard of what? Of the very things we really want to lose —our acquired negative attitudes.

Enjoyment of life is not the presence of something outside ourselves; it is the absence of something within ourselves. Gloom is a state of inner blockage of your True Self; enjoyment is its release. Just as a balloon rises to greater heights by discarding weights, so do we ascend as we toss out negativities.

How to Be Your Own Best Friend

"My daily life," said Dale F., "is like that of a caged lion. I have no will of my own. Anyone can come into the cage and make me behave as he wishes. For instance, a disturbing event comes along and I have no choice but to react with anger or gloom. I know that this affects my health, but I'm trapped. You speak a lot about the truth that sets us free. How can I find this liberating force?"

A conditioned mind can't find it at all. But you can start by being aware that you *are* conditioned. You can understand that tight nerves and sleepless nights and headaches all have their root in the False Self, in the conditioned and acquired self.

Don't make a direct effort to understand things. Rather, concentrate on your present misunderstanding. Try to see through your own false viewpoints.

Suppose you get angry at someone who offends you. The next day, you feel envious of a friend who seems luckier than you. The third day, an unexplained wave of anxiety overcomes you. The fourth day, you feel depressed because you didn't get something you wanted.

Now, you must become clearly aware of these negative states that keep you caged. See how they damage your health and drain your energy. See that they are false methods of reacting to daily events.

Be sharply aware that anger *is* false, that envy *is* pointless, that anxiety *is* harmful, that depression *is* foolish. Let me repeat a point which we emphasize in our discussions: No man ever *knowingly* harms himself with negative emotions. He does so because he is not aware of what he is doing to himself; he is hypnotized. But when he wakes up—when he sees that he is his own worst enemy—his very awareness sets him free. He then becomes his own best friend. You respond to it because deep down within yourself you sense that it is true.

How to Recognize Your Unhidden Treasure

A news item tells of a businessman in the wholesale business who handled a wide variety of items, including a few used books. Since the books played a minor role in his business, he paid them little attention. One day a friend of his, who was casually examining the stock, let loose a sharp whistle. He held up a rare volume that had been lying on dusty shelves for several months. The wholesaler learned that he owned a historical book of considerable value.

That discovery aroused the businessman's interest in rare books. He took time to study them. He now recognizes value when he sees it—and he now profits from knowing that value. [MENTAL PICTURE 55]

That is what every man and woman must do. He or she must be able to see the value in every thought or feeling or experience that comes along. As in the case of the books, it is not enough for the value to be there; it must be *recognized as value*. You must be able to mentally see your hidden treasure. Only then can you profit.

There is value in everything that happens to you, especially in those events that appear sorrowful or troublesome. Suffering can supply us with the very ending of suffering, if only we listen to its lesson. Fear, when carefully examined, can free us from fear.

I assure you that this is not a moralistic philosophy; it is an utterly practical fact. No one has expressed it more clearly than Ralph Waldo Emerson in his brilliant essay, *Compensation:*

> *Our strength grows out of our weakness. The indignation which arms itself with secret forces does not awaken until we are pricked and stung and sorely assailed. A great man is always willing to be little. Whilst he sits on the cushion of advantages, he goes to sleep. When he is pushed, tormented, defeated, he has a chance to learn something; he has been put on his wits, on his manhood; he has gained facts; learns his ignorance; he is cured of the insanity of conceit; has got moderation and real skill. The wise man throws himself on the side of his assailants. It is more his interest than it is theirs to find his weak point.*

Escape from Negative Emotions

Is it necessary to be at the mercy of painful moods and feelings? It is not. Is there a practical plan for escaping from attacks of depression, dismay, nervousness? There is.

First, remember that nature has provided no permanent housing for negative emotions within you. The negative emotional center is like an old house that everyone assumes is haunted. Because people *believe* in these inner ghosts they *act* as if the ghosts are real. The house is really empty, and if we take courage to explore it for ourselves, we will see that it is so. We will see that the so-called ghosts are the products of our own illusions! They are created by careless thinking, by uncontrolled imagination, and by imitating the frightened behavior of other haunted people.

Second, and very important, we must realize that all negative emotions are completely useless. They are more than useless; they damage the health, drain energy, and make you miserable. You must actually see the harm they do to you. As self-enlightenment dawns, your natural self-interest battles for you; it destroys them.

No one really wants to harm himself; he does so only because he doesn't really see how his negative emotions destroy his own best-interests. The motorist who anxiously tries to beat a traffic signal does so because he closes his eyes to the danger. As he *does* see it, he ceases his anxious driving. Likewise, we depart from negative moods more and more as we more and more see their damage to us.

Remember these key ideas: 1. *Negative emotions need have no permanency in your life.* 2. *Be aware of their harm.* Work with these two ideas and negativities gradually fall away.

How This Technique Will Show You There Is Nothing to Fear

I want to talk with you about the specific emotion of fear. Look around and you see a world of frightened people. Sooner or later the mask slips aside and you see fear beneath the pretense of gaiety. Look within, and if we are honest, we seen a painful collection of apprehensions and shadowy dreads.

There is nothing to fear. I know this as a fact. I want you to know it too, not as an intellectual agreement, but as a personal experience. You can *know* there is nothing to fear. I don't want you to take my word for it. I want you to follow these ideas so that you will know for yourself.

The first step is to admit honestly that you are scared. You need not identify a particular fear; it is enough to observe its haunting presence.

Then, you must be willing to be a psychological nobody. You must drop all identifications of who you are. In worldly affairs it is all right to identify yourself as a doctor or lawyer or business-man, but *psychologically, inwardly,* you must be no one at all. As long as you need to be a psychological somebody, you will be afraid. This fear comes from trying to prove that an imaginary self is real. A psychological picture we have of being a doctor or loving wife is not a reality. Fear arises as we try to prove that an outer identification—doctor or wife—has an inner reality to correspond to it. But there isn't. Fear comes when we try to prove that an imaginary self is a real self. But we cannot prove an illusion, any more than we can prove that an imaginary tree has actual branches and leaves.

Someone has asked, "I don't understand what you mean by being a psychological nobody."

I know that it is difficult to follow, so just do the best you can for now. Look at it like this: In your outer world you may be President of the United States. Inwardly, you are nothing of the sort; it is merely a means of worldly identification. When you are President as far as the exterior world is concerned, but nothing in particular in your inner world, you are at peace. It is when you think you *must* be President that you are in psychological conflict and hence afraid.

Count the Cost

At our group discussions, we actively explore the problem of negative emotions. Our purpose, of course, is to dissolve them through calling their bluff.

I want to pass on to you a technique that has proved richly beneficial to the group. It works like this: Someone reports a negative emotion that he or she permitted during the week. The negative feelings cover a wide range, including anger, superstition, pretense, pride, vanity. This person is then asked to count the cost of allowing the negative emotion to dominate his life. That provides insight for the negative person; he or she sees what a dreadful price is paid for negativity. Here is how a typical dialogue might go:

"What negative emotion did you allow last week?"
"Bitterness toward people."
"What did it cost you?"

"Oh, for one thing, plain old misery. Bitterness is a miserable state."

"Do you like being miserable?"

"No."

"Then why did you permit bitterness to take control?"

"Because I didn't count the cost."

"Well, from now on, count the cost."

Here is another:

"What negativity did you permit?"

"Several. But the worst was depression."

"Don't you know that depression is totally unnecessary? It is a stupid feature of the False Self."

"Yes. I know that."

"Then why did you fall prey to it?"

"Because I was careless in my thinking."

"Well, count the cost of that carelessness."

Try this for yourself. Try to become aware of what your negativities are costing you in the way of happiness. Remember, no man ever *consciously* harms himself. He does so because he is not consciously aware of his self-harm. By counting the cost, you awaken yourself. Then, you no longer permit negative emotions to dominate and harm you. Be sure to use this valuable exercise.

How to Avoid Negative Feelings Toward People

The story is told about a clan inhabiting the highlands of ancient Scotland. Called the Hill Clan, they had a wide reputation for fierceness. The people of the lowlands were warned to stay clear of them. The very name of Hill Clan was enough to make men tremble. Though seldom seen by the people of the lowlands, the highlanders were avoided by all.

One afternoon a band of archers lost their way while out hunting. They noticed, with apprehension, that they were in the highlands. Suddenly, someone pointed to a nearby peak and yelled, "Hill Clan!" The hunters froze in terror. Minutes later they were surrounded by a hundred Scottish highlanders.

The hunters were surprised to see the Hill Clan approach without weapons. Not only that but the highlanders held out their hands in friendly greetings.

It turned out that the Hill Clan had been completely mislabeled. They were not fierce, but peaceful. They had simply been given a false label which no one had ever questioned. Consequently, the lowlanders had lived in needless fear over the years. [MENTAL PICTURE 56]

Within this story is a rich lesson: Do not place fixed negative labels on anything. This includes events, conditions, experiences, and people. Do not call them "bad" or "painful" or "tragic." When you mechanically slap a negative label on anything you cause an emotional reaction that corresponds to the label. If you label, "I am lonely," you will feel lonely. If you insist, "This is a depressing situation," you instantly activate the emotion of gloom—and suffer from it.

Don't label. *See the event or experience as something entirely separate from your attitude toward it.* Be neutral. Don't personalize. Don't add your judgment. Detach your opinion. I assure you that this can be done. It is what people with inner peace do as a matter of course. That is why they are able to handle each daily event with quiet power.

Summary: By refusing to label, you prevent negative feelings from arising and harming you. You see the event in a totally new and surprising way. The process is like removing the thorns from a rose. It leaves you with something pleasant, not something frightening.

Using the Magical Word to Brighten Every Gloomy Situation

Let me give you a word with magical meaning. It is one you should remember whenever you wonder whether you are getting anywhere or not. This magical word is *comparison.*

How do you know whether one automobile is better than another? The only possible way to find out is to compare the two. How can you tell whether you are getting anywhere in your piano lessons? The only way is to see whether you play a bit better today than you did yesterday. Again, your accurate guide is comparison.

In your life-growth you must use frank comparison to see whether you are really rolling forward. If not, you can then question your technique or your information or your teachers.

You must be forthright about it. You must say, "If I am not making genuine progress, if I am not a bit more free of negativity today than yesterday, then something must be wrong." Your self-honesty enables you to identify false trails and abandon them.

Here is the real tragedy of mankind. A man rarely stops to inquire whether there might be something better than his suffering. He seldom pauses in his worrisome pursuit of money to see whether he might make just as much money without all that worry. In his agony over losing a certain woman, he doesn't see the possibility of losing that woman without also losing his sanity. The needless tragedy is that he has no sense of alternatives.

The man who dares to challenge the false power of a dark condition will not fail to win. Even a small effort gives him a glimpse of alternatives, shows him the difference between his pain and his freedom from it. He is like a man in a dark cavern who finds a small candle to light. That small candle will not illuminate the whole cave, but it gives him a basis for comparison. He sees, ever so dimly, that *there is an alternative to darkness.* Having seen that much, he eagerly lights another candle and another and another, until he finds himself in the bright light. He is no longer afraid of the cavern because he now sees and understands it. [MENTAL PICTURE 57]

Compare last week with this week. If you find you are making progress, make more. If you discover yourself spinning in circles, apply the principles of Psycho-Pictography.

TO END EMOTIONAL TROUBLES

1. Use your vast force of attention.
2. Learn to detach yourself mentally from surrounding storms.
3. Remember the lessons taught by Don Quixote.
4. Work at uplifting your feelings by revising your mental viewpoints. It works.

5. Be your own best friend by understanding the facts about negative emotions.

6. When met and handled rightly, present suffering frees you from future suffering. Here is a challenge!

7. Remember, *always remember,* that there is no permanent housing for any negative emotion.

8. Review the section entitled, "How This Technique Will Show You There Is Nothing to Fear."

9. Don't label experiences as being painful. Withdraw the label and you withdraw the pain.

10. Remember the magical word *comparison.* It is bright light.

10

Release Your Full Mental Powers for Greater Success

What do you suppose would happen to your world if you mentally saw it as another world?

Something would happen all right. Something magically marvelous. You would live in a bright world that turns for your pleasure and enrichment.

Let's explore this world together, for as Plato explained, "My mind is myself. To take care of myself is to take care of my mind."

The man who really understands his mental processes is the man who can use them to attain any worthwhile goal. But the person who fails to explore his potentialities of mental power will needlessly remain as he is. We must start with the idea that we have many exciting things to learn and to understand. With that receptive attitude, we cannot fail.

When these ideas were presented at a group discussion, someone asked, "What are some of the things we must understand?

Could we discuss practical examples of how right thinking aids our everyday progress?"

Here are some of the helpful points brought out:

> *Like an eagle, your mind was created to soar.*
>
> *Do not involve yourself in other people's problems merely to distract your mind from your own.*
>
> *To fail to understand something does not mean that your mind must go on to misunderstand it.*
>
> *There is no outer progress without inner mental change.*
>
> *You are becoming a mental magician when you control not only what you want to do, but also what you don't want to do.*
>
> *We must cease to know so many things that are untrue.*
>
> *Like successfully working a crossword puzzle, mental power reveals itself steadily and gradually.*

Fully understood, any one of the above ideas could transport you to the mountain-top, where everything is clear.

How to Fly to Peaks of Mental Awareness

Nothing is more certain than that the human mind possesses ten times the power usually used. Why does the average person fail to express his maximum mental might?

The answer is his *lack of awareness.* A man simply doesn't take time for an exploration that could make these forces consciously known to him. Instead of pausing to study the magic of his mind, he casually assumes that what he now sees is all that there is. That is like thinking that the first edge of dawn is all there is to the sun! Don't make this mistake. We can assist our understanding with an illustration:

Suppose you were given a one-man airplane to use in any way you like. But you did not understand the powers of an airplane; you were unaware that it could carry you across the sky. But still, wanting to make some use of it, you hitched it to a horse and drove it around. Because of your limited awareness of its use, your actual use was also limited. But after studying the machine for a while you discover its motor, propeller, and other items of power. So you unhitch the horse and drive the airplane around on the ground with its own power. This is an advanced use, but still far from making the most of its intended purpose. So you study some more and you discover that the airplane has wings for a practical purpose; you see the possibilities of rising above the earth to soar aloft. With this new knowledge you go into action. Finally, you fly. By discovering the full capacities of that airplane, it carries you to whatever destinations you desire. [MENTAL PICTURE 58]

A man's mind is like that. The power is there all right, blocked only by lack of awareness that it *is* there. Persistent self-study reveals power that is already there. Your very awareness is your power for full flight.

How to Get Off the Mental Merry-Go-Round

Have you ever wished that you could blot out your mind and cease to think about things? Ever wish to jump off the mental merry-go-round that takes you nowhere? People would often give anything to shut off the frantic chasing of their thoughts.

This desire to stop thinking proves something. It proves that we recognize the futility of fighting life with the inadequate weapons of habitual, conditioned, and shallow thoughts. Thought has its place, but it is really a secondary power. *There is something far superior.*

The fact is, you can and you should stop thinking with your tradition-formed mind! Old, fixed, personalized, and biased thinking patterns get you nowhere—as every man proves to himself a dozen times a day.

What, then, is the replacement for conditioned thinking?

Awareness. Here is the supreme secret.

It is essential that you see the vast difference between *thought* and *awareness.* This is an advanced lesson in unleashing your full mental powers, and because it is, you can advance swiftly with it.

What, exactly, is *thought?* First, it is our memory in action. If our memory stocks the opinion that life is unfair, we will project this opinion wherever we go—and be unhappy. In other words, thought is mere repetition, just as a newspaper headline is repeated with each roll of the press. Also, thought can be utterly mistaken. Our thoughts are based on our conditioning during our early years. If bitter people told us that life is unfair, our impressionable minds accepted that as a fact. But it is not a fact;

it is the False Self feeling sorry for itself. Thinking is based on acquired viewpoints and attitudes which may not be in line with reality.

When we merely think about something, we could be wrong; but when we are aware of something, we are never wrong, for awareness is a revelation of the truth about that something.

Perhaps this helps you to understand why all your thinking about your problems has never solved them. Thinking goes in a maddening circle, getting you nowhere.

Now, thought is both good and necessary for the mechanical processes of life, like building a house or cooking dinner. But because your spiritual self is not mechanical, it must be elevated by an entirely different power. That power is *awareness*.

Don't Be Afraid to Be Without an Attitude

Let's take an interesting example of the difference between thought and awareness:

Suppose that you decide to take a vacation, say, at a resort in the heights of the Rocky Mountains. You send away for literature which you read eagerly. And you *think about* that resort. You wonder what it's really like, you hope it's a fun-place and so on. But, of course, you can't do any more than to merely think about it, to repeatedly speculate. And that speculation neither answers your questions nor gives you pleasure. No, you realize that you must actually travel to that higher level, you must explore the place itself.

So you journey to the resort. Now, everything is utterly different. You no longer *think about* the place; you are *clearly aware of it as it actually is*. You may even see that many of your previous speculations were not in line with the revealed reality. Yes, for the first time, you really know the truth! Thinking has ended, awareness has begun. And because you are now on a higher level, you can really enjoy yourself. [MENTAL PICTURE 59]

Spend some time reflecting upon the difference between thought and awareness. It makes a vast difference in your life.

Suppose you work long and hard at your desk in the office. You feel that you deserve a promotion. But when the time comes to fill a vacancy, someone else gets it. You are hurt and angry.

You indignantly feel that there is no justice in the world. As a result of your reaction, you suffer. Now let me ask you a question: Who caused you to suffer?

Here is where we must be very wise. The situation itself—you must try to see this—the situation itself had no power to hurt you. You injured yourself by your very own thoughts about it. You see, you wanted this promotion very badly. Why? Believe it or not, it wasn't for the money primarily. You wanted to prove something to yourself and to your family; for example, that you were efficient, loyal, worthy, and so on. When this need—which is part of the False Self—was thwarted, you felt resentful, grieved. Proving yourself is a needless need.

It is the False Self with all its demands, fears, egotisms, and illusions that tries to prove itself. But you *can't* prove an illusion. It is like trying to fill a bottomless jar. When you find your True Self, you need not try to prove anything. When you discover that you are really a millionaire, need you prove it? When you know your True Self, which is content in every situation, you are never upset, promotion or not.

You will find abundant enrichment as you remember:

You need not work at thinking, at trying to find the right attitude toward something that happens to you. The problem arises because you *have* an attitude, a needless one. *Dare to be without an attitude.*

Make this experiment: Go about your normal affairs without thinking and planning and choosing quite so frantically. Don't strain for right attitudes. Instead of trying to force the river of events to flow, let the flow carry you forward. Let your thoughts twist and turn as they will. *But watch them as they flow.* What a dawning! You will do everything just as well as when you worked so hard at thinking—in fact, much better. Your business affairs, your health, your social relations, and especially your emotional life will swing upward. Best of all, you will begin to think in a new way. You will be an aware person. And an aware person is happy, natural, at rest.

Yes, it takes heroism to let your mind perform in its own natural way. But why not be a hero? Why not leave your mental processes to their own abundant wisdom? One of the first exclamations you will then make is a grateful, "What a relief!"

How You Can Break Free From Weighty Worries

I often hear questions like:

"Why do I find it so difficult to break even the smallest habit?"

"Is there really a way to crash through into the new life you tell us about?"

"Is there some sort of unseen resistance that prevents us from helping ourselves?"

By exploring a few special facts, you can find positive answers to questions like these. I want to supply you with these special facts. They may be the very ones you have been seeking for many years. Once seen and understood, they banish dozens of dusty difficulties, just as a brisk wind clears the air of dust.

The following Mental Picture is designed especially to help you understand certain facts about the human situation:

At amusement parks they have motor boats that glide around a lake or lagoon with their load of passengers. Each boat has a park employee who serves as captain and guide. Although he stands at the wheel as if steering the boat, he really doesn't. He has no control over the boat's course as it weaves left and right around the lagoon.

What, then, controls the boat's direction? A set of rails, out of sight beneath the surface of the water. The boat merely follows—it *must* follow—these underwater rails. Day after day, trip after trip, it follows mechanically along as the rails dictate. [MENTAL PICTURE 60]

This is a good example of how the majority of men and women live. They seem to be gliding happily around the lagoons of life, but they are not really happy, nor are they in control of themselves. For beneath the surface of their lives, they are controlled and enslaved by their mental negative rails. Because they do not understand that this is so, they fail in even the tiniest task. No matter how hard a man may try to control his temper, he fails. Even when a woman doesn't want to be carried along by a jealous mood, she cannot resist it. Because they do not realize what is controlling them, they remain in secret despair.

But there is a great truth that every man and woman can realize: *There is a way to break free!* Past mistakes need not harm your present life. You need not react to any crisis with distress or confusion. You can cease all mechanical, daily trips that keep you nervous or helpless or frightened.

I know for a fact that any man can be free of all negativities. He can behave in a new way. He can think from a fresh mind. He can have pleasurable days, filled with exciting discoveries.

The underwater mental rails consist of frozen attitudes, unrealistic conclusions, habitual thoughts, compulsive desires. Now, most people simply do not realize that their attitudes *are* frozen and unrealistic, they do not see that their ideas about themselves are habitual but not necessarily correct. Instead, they think that their attitudes are the only ones that exist, and therefore must be the correct ones. But this is incorrect; destructively incorrect.

We must break the false power of these mental rails.

Where can we start? With the knowledge that those restricting rails are down there, that they are the cause of our troubles. Most people do not know this. They do not see what is going on beneath the surface of their lives. But you now know it. This knowledge is a powerful tool. To see that we are not presently free is the beginning of eventual freedom. This is really great news. It is cause for good cheer.

Especially try to see the harm caused by these negative rails. See that they are the cause of your distress. This comes as a gradual revelation. As it does, you see more clearly how to disengage yourself from them. The boat, when free of its underwater rails, can go anywhere and enjoy anything. Likewise, when you are free of subconscious negativities, you live the fancy-free life.

How to Move Over to a Great New Life

A useful illustration popped up while I was going through a copy of Daniel Defoe's classic, *Robinson Crusoe*. Shipwrecked on an isolated island, Robinson Crusoe made his camp near the place where he came ashore. He then set about to explore his private kingdom. It wasn't long before he made a discovery that threw him into conflict. He found that he was camped on the wrong side of the island. The other side had a greater abundance of food and comfort. Though seeing the fact clearly, he was reluctant to move. [MENTAL PICTURE 61]

Why? Why not exchange the less for the more, the inferior for the superior? Since anyone can find a richer life, how come so many miss it?

There are a number of reasons why people fail to move over to their richer world. Mental idleness is one. Lack of persistence. Searching in the wrong places. Getting discouraged at the slightest setback. Fear of change.

Let me give you a reason which people rarely suspect. They fear that fresh ideas will rob them of their habitual ways, of their settled comfort. They are afraid to reach for more for fear of losing what little they have. Here is where courage is needed. We must abandon the old before we can find the new.

Does that apply to our emotional habits?

Very much so. Suppose a person habitually lives with a certain negative emotion, for instance, depression. This may startle you, but such a person resists the idea of giving up his depression. As painful as it is, he won't give it up. Why? It supplies him with a false sense of identity; that is, he can say, "Well, at least I know who I am—I am a depressed person." He fears giving up that painful emotion because he fears his loss of identity as a depressed person. Also, strangely enough, some people take a great pride in being negative; for instance, a man will boast of his bad temper.

Remember the illustration of Robinson Crusoe's reluctance to move to the brighter side of the island. Do you see what you must do?

Learn to Judge Things by Results

Here is a good place to answer a question that goes like this: I don't know what set of ideas to follow in order to find myself. In the past I have studied several religions and philosophies. Now I have a new one. How can I tell whether it has real value?

There is one sure way. By results. By *actual results*. The seeker must be ruthlessly honest with himself about the outcomes of his studies. If genuine freedoms are not appearing, he must courageously face it. No man can find his way out of prison if he insists that he is not imprisoned.

Challenge the set of ideas you use. Demand, yes, make an outright demand that they prove themselves by giving you something new, something better, something happier. If the system you use is honest, it will not only welcome your challenge but encourage it. Truthful systems are never afraid of anything because they are not hiding anything.

Challenge your ideas. Do this by habitually asking yourself questions like:

> Do I see definite changes in the way I think, feel, act, and speak?
> Am I really a bit happier each week?
> Is this system a practical aid toward altering my inner self from negative to positive?

The supreme test comes when you first suspect that a system is not keeping its promise to you. At this point, you must courageously abandon it, even while unsure of its replacement. If you will daringly set sail upon uncharted seas, you will find the only safe harbor there is—the Truth itself.

How to Use These Ideas

The way you meet a fresh idea is of utmost importance. If you shy away from a new truth because it is difficult to understand or because it is strange, you cannot gain its value. Also, if you assume that you already understand the full significance of a fresh thought, you likewise cut yourself off from its hidden treasure.

When you encounter a new idea, perhaps in this book, do not start off by accepting or rejecting it. Do not react automatically to it. You must walk around and over the new territory to see whether it has gold or not. *You must not take anyone's word for anything.* You must personally prove all offered plans and techniques. You must reason, "If it really works, it will prove itself sooner or later. I will give it a chance to reveal its value." That is the intelligent way to separate fact from fiction, truth from falsehood.

The process can be likened to selecting a map that you wish to guide you toward a desired destination. Suppose that you want to travel to Ohio. You select a map from the library shelf and examine it. If it covers the state of Ohio, you look at it more closely, you study details. But if it covers another state, you set it aside. But your first act is to take a clear look at the selected map; you neither accept nor reject it without personal examination. You accept or reject it only when your own intelligence tells you whether or not it serves your need. [MENTAL PICTURE 62]

Once you discover a psychological idea of definite worth to you, use the following plans to increase your benefits:

1. Look for its deeper significance, its greater value.
2. Frequently reflect upon it in your spare moments and as you go about your usual tasks.
3. Bring it up for discussion in your study group, such as at a Psycho-Pictography meeting, outlined in Chapter 15.
4. Write it down on a slip of paper for easy reference.
5. Make it your goal to understand the idea with maximum clarity.
6. Do not hesitate to insert the new idea into the place of an unworkable one.
7. Discuss it with other people who show an interest in its value.
8. Work at using the idea in a practical way in your business or employment, in your home, in human relations.

Start Taking Orders from Headquarters and Get Somewhere

Follow the eight plans simply and easily. One of man's greatest illusions is that hard work in itself is a virtue. Only *right* work is virtuous. And right work is easy and effortless. As we get out of our own way, this easy-going progress becomes a cheery reality.

We spoke of the need to separate fact from fancy. Nothing can do more for you than to see the difference between the real and the unreal. *Whatever is real is beneficial; whatever is false is harmful.* We are on the way to greater mental health and to physical well-being as we discern the difference between the truth about life and what we mistakenly take as truth.

A colonel told his officers that their army must take a strongly fortified enemy position. A captain pointed out the problems of the order and asked why it had to be done. "Because," replied the colonel, "it's an order from headquarters."

A truthful idea is an order from your inner headquarters—

your True Self. Although it may originate from a book or a speaker, it must be matched by your consent. When that happens, a magnificent miracle happens to you.

How Help Arrives When You Connect with Your True Self

Historians praise the marvelous system of communications set up by the ancient Roman Empire. They agree that Rome's ability to keep in touch with its far-flung territories gave it solid strength. The communications were achieved by setting up a network of roads and signal stations that connected Rome with its provinces. A need for troops in Egypt was swiftly communicated to Rome and the troops rushed out. A call for engineers from far-away Britain was answered promptly with the necessary manpower. The roads between the well-supplied headquarters and the outer regions were open and ready. [MENTAL PICTURE 63]

Let that form a picture of how your mind can supply your needs, wherever the call. See your mind as permanent headquarters which can swiftly send out wisdom, understanding, strength, cheer.

This is really more than a picture. It is a fact. What bountiful supplies arrive to the man who maintains clear communications between his inner self and his exterior affairs!

Take the understanding of a so-called bothersome event—for instance, a sarcastic remark from someone. One man was asked why he remained unaffected by such a remark. He replied, "Because it makes a difference only if I think it does—and I don't think it does."

The daily power of such an intelligent man is clearly described by Dr. Paul Brunton:

Thus, living as close to the Divine Centre as he can, he may still be able to take his appropriate place in the world, no longer as its slave, but as Nature's co-operator. Whilst his inmost being dwells in a strange spirituality, he himself will be able to move in the very midst of stress and tumult, not blind to its existence or indifferent to its problems, but nevertheless inwardly poised and untroubled. Therefore he can cope more effectively with these problems. He has found that at that centre—whether of self or the universe—there dwells real safety and sanity.[1]

How to Make Profitable Decisions

You are about to receive an entirely new method for making daily decisions. It will abolish strained thinking and worried wondering over the course to take. Every day includes dozens of decisions, ranging from trivial to vital. Why not make profitable decisions every time? It can be done.

We start by looking into an enormous fact of human existence. *It is possible for you to think with a new mind.*

This new mind is free of doubt and perplexity. It never makes a wrong decision. Just as a well-kept garden is free of weeds and stones, so is this new mind free of doubts and confusions. It *knows* what to do. It shows you the difference between a profitable action and a pointless one. It prevents you from doing or saying things that you would later regret. It keeps you out of trouble. Not only does it tell you what to do, but what *not* to do.

Understand this: Most decisions are made on the basis of desire. You do this or that because you want something out of it. But if this desire is unrealistic, or risky to your welfare, you head for grief. But when you think with your new mind, one that is free of illusion and impulsiveness, *you don't have self-defeating desires.* So you solve the problem of decision by not creating the decision in the first place! I assure you that this is a magical way to live.

Take the spending of money—when you think clearly about your *real* needs, you spend your money wisely. You buy things for practical reasons, not for shallow ego-gratification. So, thinking from a clear mind is really a raise in pay.

A woman told me about the man in her life, then asked, "Should I marry him or not?"

I tried to explain that a decision based in a muddled mind is not only risky but needless. "Why not," I advised, "put first things first? Clear up your thinking—which you can certainly do —and then you will know exactly what to do."

---

[1] Paul Brunton, *The Quest of the Overself* (New York: E. P. Dutton and Co. Inc., 1938).

The intelligent person ignores what to *do*. He concentrates on what to *be*. We must put first things first. To be clear-minded is first. Obviously, that is the only kind of mind that makes accurate and profitable decisions.

The principles of Psycho-Pictography guide you toward your new and clear mind.

FOR YOUR TOTAL MIND-POWER

1. Have confidence in your ability to develop maximum mental might.
2. You need not ride the pointless mental merry-go-round.
3. The supreme secret for breaking out of the circle of problems is *awareness*.
4. Work at seeing the vast difference between thought and awareness. It is a heroic adventure of endless rewards.
5. Replace a strained effort at thinking with a quiet awareness of everything that goes on.
6. Break away from frozen attitudes and acquired convictions. It leads to the fancy-free life.
7. Like Robinson Crusoe, you can move over to the superior life!
8. Demand practical results from any system that tells you how to live.
9. Learn to take orders from your inner headquarters— your True Self. It supplies accurate guidance.
10. As you learn to think with a new mind, daily decisions become easy and profitable.

11

Say Good-Bye to Fear
and Tension

Picture a man lost in the woods. Dusk is descending and the dangers of the dark creep in. The man knows that a false step might drop him into a deep pit or treacherous marsh. Wild animals lurk in the shadows. A storm threatens.

Suddenly, the lost man sights another struggling wanderer. He asks for the way out. The stranger offers immediate and friendly help. After following the stranger for a while, the lost man realizes that his supposed guide is just as lost as he is. So he parts company, to set out once more on his own. Soon, he comes across a second stranger who confidently claims to possess an accurate map of the escape route. The lost man follows this new counselor, but again it becomes obvious that the man is self-deceived and that his map is a pathetic result of his self-deception. The lost man wanders on in deepening despair. He runs into others who claim knowledge of the way out, but he sees from the half-concealed distress in their eyes that they are just as lost as he.

Then, as he stumbles about, the wanderer places his hand into his coat pocket for warmth. His fingers curl about something hard and reassuring. He withdraws a compass. He laughs with comfort and relief as he realizes that it was there all along. He had only to look within himself. He had been so busy inquiring of others, that he had failed to do the one necessary thing. But now he has found his salvation within himself. [MENTAL PICTURE 64]

Like that wanderer, you have an inner compass to guide you from the forest of dread and dismay. And I am not speaking philosophically or from mere theory. It is a fact that emotional fear is unnecessary. If anyone tells you otherwise, that person has not yet found himself.

The answer to fear exists, but we must not give in to easy answers. We must never surrender our individuality and our integrity to another person merely because that person claims to know the answer. We must and we can find it for ourselves. Even our despair can aid us, as Dr. Paul Tillich points out:

> For in the depth of every serious doubt and every despair of truth, the passion for truth is still at work. Don't give in too quickly to those who want to alleviate your anxiety about truth. Don't be seduced into a truth which is not really your truth . . .[1]

The Only Way to Be Unafraid

People want to identify fear, explore it, find ways to get rid of it once and for all. So let's examine it for ourselves.

Is it really possible to abolish daily anxiety?

Yes, certainly. Personally, I *know* that it is quite possible. However, there is no way I can convince you of this with mere words. You cannot know my state; you can only know your own. But your own state can eventually rise to the level where you are wonderfully unafraid.

First we should realize that we are not talking about a fear having a realistic basis in the outer world. If you are afraid when crossing a busy street or when chased by a tiger, that is a realistic fear. It is self-protective, insures survival. But we are talking about inner fears, that is, those vague, nagging, and painful anxieties that you can't quite identify or understand.

---

[1] Paul Tillich, *The New Being* (New York: Charles Scribner's Sons, 1955).

Fear is a part of every negative emotion. Anger is based on fear. Bitterness extends from a frightened state of mind. Loneliness is quite obviously a fear of being alone. The depressed person is frightened. And so on.

Let's go back to the original question, *what is fear?* You must follow this very closely. We are diving deeply into the problem. I assure you that your careful exploration is the means of freedom from a quivering mind. You know very well that you have previously tried many systems and philosophies and plans that haven't worked. You are still very much afraid. But if you will grasp all this as best you can, you will come out nicely. Once you really understand, you will be free.

Understand the Secret of Inner Freedom

Here we go. Simply stated, a man is afraid because he suspects that he is really not the false images he has built up about himself. In reality, he is *not* these false images, but he wants to believe that he is. All inner fear is founded on trying to believe that an illusion is a reality.

Everyone has imaginary ideas of himself as being this or that sort of person. And you can be sure that the images are highly complimentary! But since they are purely imaginary, they are highly sensitive to assault by reality.

By way of illustration, a young lady once told me, "The other day I was upset by being told that I had a dull personality. Was that because I had a picture of myself as having a bright personality?"

"Right. Otherwise you would not have been upset. You see, you have the false notion that it is good to have a bright and bouncy personality. Why is it good? You think it's good because you envy people who go around appearing to be very gay and enthusiastic. What you don't know is that they are very miserable when the show is over, when they are all alone. Why try to have a bright personality? Why not just be yourself? Whether you know it or not, a *real* personality is ten times more attractive than a bright one."

To sum up: You have certain imaginary ideas about the kind of a person that you are. You get scared whenever anyone or anything threatens to expose them for the illusions that they are. You will resent anyone who tells you the truth about them. But it is the exposure of these illusions that sets you free.

Why, then, do you resist so fiercely the unmasking of your false self-images?

Because you are afraid that by losing them you will also lose your identity. Since they make up the only identity you know, you are terrified that their loss will mean the loss of *you*. But—and listen carefully to this—it is the loss of this False Self that enables you to discover who you really are! You must have the courage to drop the False Self—as temporarily frightening as it may be—in order to find the True Self.

Once you become aware of all the phony images of the False Self, they fall away. This creates a psychological vacuum which is quickly filled by the True Self. And your True Self is beautifully free of fear.

Free Yourself from Fear by Following Your Clues a Step at a Time

An adventure story revolved around a man who found a small section of a treasure map. The section hinted of a fabulous treasure and supplied a single clue for locating it. The man tried to find more sections, but failed. Deciding to use what little he had of the map, he took the first step of sailing for an island in the West Indies. There, among some rocks in a cove, he found a second section. He followed its directions to a grove of trees, where a third piece was found. So step by step, from one clue to the next, he went on to locate the treasure. [MENTAL PICTURE 65]

There is a rich lesson here, namely, we need take only one easy step at a time. In our search for inner liberation, we need do only whatever we can do at the present moment. It is a mistake to try to act above our present level of understanding; it is correct to do whatever is possible for the time, as elementary as it may be.

One valuable step is to become aware of a specific worry or tension. This puts spotlights on it, gives you something definite to observe and study. During a Psycho-Pictography session, a woman told of her specific stress:

"I am afraid of other people being angry with me. I don't want to displease them for fear they'll flare up at me. It must be a carry-over from girlhood; I can think of several people who were always mad at me. It terrified me. I tried to keep their anger down by doing what they wanted me to do. I felt that it was wrong to please them like this, but I was too scared to rebel. Today, I still have the same awful pressure. I still do things I really don't want to do. I'm afraid to speak and act the way I honestly feel. I've told myself a thousand times that I'm sacrificing my inner integrity, but I'm still chained. How can I break the chains?"

She accomplished a good deal for herself simply by bringing the problem out into the open before the group. That was a sensible and healthy first step. It was simply a matter of more time and insight that finally set her free.

What can you do right now? What simple step would help you at this very moment. I suggest that you review some ideas or paragraphs in these pages that have special meaning for you. They are accurate clues that lead to your treasure of abundant living.

How to Handle the Future

"I have a lurking dread of the future," admitted my caller. "Is there anything I can do about it? I seem to have a subconscious nagging over what will happen to me tomorrow. How can I plan future events with calm wisdom?"

Have you ever noticed how things always turn out differently from the way you plan them, no matter how wisely? You rehearse a forthcoming event in your mind, such as a business conference or a romantic meeting with the opposite sex. You plan what to say, the tone of voice you will use, the way you will act. You even go so far as to imagine the reactions of the other person. Yet, when the event occurs, it bears no resemblance to the imagined version. So you get confused and troubled.

But when nothing happens as expected, we are lost. Don't set up fixed ideas as to how things *should* happen. Just let them happen in any way they like; don't force a thing. Maintain an inner flexibility. Then, whatever happens, you are able to handle it.

That is the very thing that carries you through every challenge. You see, we set up these fixed plans as protective armor, but they are no armor at all. The slightest unexpected word or facial expression from the other person can penetrate it, causing pain. But when you heroically expect *anything, nothing* hurts!

Suppose you are playing tennis. You don't expect the ball to come from this direction or that. You don't assume the other player will hit the ball for your convenience. To play with such fixed assumptions would cost you the game. Instead, you let the ball come as it will, then meet it in whatever way is best. This flexibility supplies skill for returning each and every ball. Be just as flexible toward everything that happens to you in the future, large events or small. That is how to win the game. [MENTAL PICTURE 66]

How to Escape from Any and All Fears

One evening during a group discussion, we were talking over the third of the **Four Golden Keys** supplied in Chapter 1, that of self-honesty. "I'd like," someone said, "a good example of how self-sincerity helps us."

"All right," I replied, "take the problem of fright. Everyone is far more fearful than he likes to admit to himself or to others. People like to put on a good front, but it doesn't cover their secret anxieties. Their faces tell their fears." I then requested, "Search yourselves right now. Tell me, honestly, what frightens you?" A variety of apprehensions were exposed:

"I'm afraid of making decisions."
"I worry over world affairs."
"Financial problems."
"Guilt and fear over past mistakes."
"I dread ill-health."
"I don't know who I am."
"A feeling of helplessness."
"I'm anxious over the future."
"I'm afraid of being disliked."
"Just an underground anxiety in general."

There is not a fear in this list that cannot be canceled from anyone's life. There is no other fear that might be added that cannot be banished entirely from anyone's day.

Whenever you are afraid of anything, remember, first of all, that there *is* a way out. It exists. It makes no difference whether you are presently aware of it or not; it still exists. This is a powerful idea to keep in mind. A man mistakenly assumes that his unawareness of something is the same thing as the non-existence of that something. But this is like assuming that an Egyptian pyramid doesn't exist merely because we haven't seen it as yet. We must not assume that our non-awareness of something is the same thing as its non-existence.

So there are ways out. Here is one of them:

Whenever you fear a person or circumstance, ask yourself, "Just *who* is afraid? Exactly *who* is this fearful self?" Question the identity of the self that gets frightened. The answer can be the greatest revelation of your life. It is always the False Self that falls victim to dread and despair, but in reality, *you are not your False Self*.

This needs exploration and review. You have a True Self and a False Self. All mental fear—and this means *all* mental fear—springs from the False Self. Only this conditioned False Self is fearful of atom bombs and of social disapproval and of past mistakes. When a man thinks from this False Self, he fears everything.

But you need not think from this terrifying position. You can disengage yourself from it. You can begin to see that your fears are founded upon the illusions and unrealities and deceits and follies of the False Self. You can begin to see the difference between the False Self, which is always afraid, and the True Self, which is never afraid.

In other pages we covered the problem of identification. To identify with something means that you take it as being *you*. But you are not your name, or your physical body, or your position, or money. All these are mere attachments which have nothing to do with the essential self.

You are not your painful thoughts; therefore, you need not be pained by them. You are not your depressing emotions; therefore, you need never be depressed. You are not your physical body; therefore, you need not be concerned with either handsomeness or plainness.

Do not try to discover who you really are. Try to see who you are *not*. You are not the things you identify with, that you attach yourself to, that you possess. Once you see who you are not, you will know who you really are. And you will experience an utterly new kind of inner peace.

Do not be concerned if this is not entirely clear to you as yet. Grasp it as best you can for now. You have made a good start; that is all that is necessary for now. Read and review these ideas. Gradually, clarity and understanding will come. And with them will come a new sense of release and relief.

How the Return to Your True Self Ends Fear

To return to the basic idea, you must see that there is a difference between your True Self and your False Self. The True Self is the essential you. It is pure, unconditioned, natural, spiritual. It has nothing to do with ego-competition, pretense, self-deception, pride, vanity, arrogance, and other negativities that keep a man afraid. All such items belong to the False Self. The New Testament refers to it as the old nature, while a modern psychologist would call it the ego-self which is imprisoned by its own illusions, which it takes as realities.

You may ask, "Does a return to the True Self guarantee the end of fear?"

Absolutely. Take this idea as entirely practical. Apply it to any area of your life you like—your business matters, social affairs, love life, and sex concerns. You will see that it works. I must tell you something else. It is the *only* thing that *does* work. You must make up your mind to search it out for yourself. Otherwise, you will continue to pay the price of fear.

Suppose you want a certain person but cannot have him. By finding your True Self, you will then be free of the fearful heartache.

Let's see how it works. You desire this person. Why? Because he supplies your False Self with certain ego-satisfactions; for example, you think he is charming, you think he gives you a sense of acceptance, of self-worth, and so on. So you yearn for him. If you can't have him, you suffer. Why do you suffer? Because your False Self is deprived of its illusions of self-worth. That other person, in himself, means nothing to you. You are attracted by your own false ideals about him. As you see that these self-projected glorifications are part of the False Self, the other person loses his appeal for you. He never had them in the first place. They originated in your own insecure mind.

How to Avoid the Horror Films in Your Everyday Life

Suppose you slip out of bed some morning with the resolve to make it a cheery day. You determine to think and do nothing but bright and constructive things.

Then you walk to the television set and turn it on—to a horror film. You sit down to watch mad monsters tear up the earth. You see nothing but vicious destruction.

Now, turning on that horror film is something you would not do if you had resolved to make it a peaceful day.

Yet, that is exactly what millions of people do every morning. They start their day with their own horror film. And it is an endless performance; it runs deep into the night.

That horror film is in the mind. We call it *negative imagination*. It is really a horrible way to go through the day. [MENTAL PICTURE 67]

Negative imagination is a chief barrier to creative living. But —and here is great news—the dismissal of negative imagination is a chief contribution to peaceful days. Here again we have the principle that happiness is a ridding process; tranquility arrives as we *lose our negativities*, not as we acquire anything.

We can be off to a good start simply by being aware that we are actually running a horror film through our minds. We need, at the start, merely to notice it, to become aware that it is on the screen. We should notice how we mentally picture people being unkind to us, not appreciating us, threatening us, and so on.

Having done this, we can now see one thing very clearly: it is not actually happening, we are only *thinking it is happening*. But that is enough to cause pain.

Remember, you are *not* your negative thoughts. You are *not* your painful imaginations. See yourself as separate from your thoughts. This will aid you in dismissing the horror films. Just as fire fades when not fed additional fuel, so do emotional fires fade away when we cease to fuel them with negative imagination.

How to Start Each Day with a Tranquil Mind

A clear mind is a peaceful mind. Marcus Aurelius—that rare combination of Roman emperor and philosopher—phrased it like this: "By a tranquil mind I mean nothing else than a well-ordered mind."

How can a man or woman start the quest for a clear and a tranquil mind? There is no better way than to ponder these two great truths:

1. There is a way out.
2. Any sincere seeker can find it.

The way out of *what*? Out of the psychological prison that every individual dimly realizes he is within. It is a prison with endless cells, one of fear, another of anxiety, a third of the painful feeling that one has been cheated out of the best of life—and on and on. There is a way out of every one of these cells of desperation.

To take a specific instance, Steve G. was puzzled and commented, "I heard you say that we shouldn't feel guilty over our mistakes. I know that in the past I've been unkind, even cruel to people. Wouldn't guilt be a natural reaction to this? Why shouldn't I feel guilty?"

For several reasons, one of them being that guilt is a purely self-centered emotion. It supplies an unhealthy thrill to condemn yourself, to reflect about your cruel self. But let's concentrate on the most important reason why you must abolish guilt from your life. It is a familiar but totally false idea that guilt is a sign of humility or repentance. Far from producing humility, it creates the exact opposite. Being a miserable pressure, a sense of guilt drives the individual into *more* negativity, such as arrogance, hostility, and additional cruelty. Such cruelty may be rationalized and covered up, either slyly or openly, but it is still there. So a sense of guilt leads to hostile actions that produce more guilt. A person in such a condition is caught up in the vicious circle so well known to psychiatrists and psychologists.

The way out, then, is to understand the whole process of guilt.

How to Stop Fighting with Yourself

Every once in awhile the newspapers report the strange case of a soldier who didn't know the war was over. One such case was a Japanese infantryman who was still jungle-fighting World War II some 15 years after the surrender. When approached by friendly forces, the soldier staged a one-man attack. It took several days to convince the frightened veteran that peace had been declared long ago. When he finally understood, he laid down his rifle and went peacefully home. [MENTAL PICTURE 68]

Man might be likened to such a bewildered soldier. Out of touch with the realities of the spiritual world, surrounded by fear and hostility, he continues to fight. Not knowing that the war is over, that peace has already been won for him, he battles daily, even with those who bring him the message of peace. No wonder his world is a fearful jungle!

Take the individual who fights for power in the political, social, or business world. Even if he wins a skirmish or a battle, he is surprised to find that he is really no happier than he was before. In his shaking shock he mistakenly reasons, "Well, if personal power doesn't fill me, it must be something else." So off he goes to battle for great wealth or sexual conquest or community recognition. And each campaign, even when ending in victory, brings him greater despair than before. The very conquest that he counted on for inner satisfaction only deepens his dread.

Such a man must understand that he can never win this kind of war. He must see that the war he really wants to win—the one over his own compulsive desires—is already won. He need only listen to the message of victory from the True Self within. In that receptive state he will happily see that he has no need to fight for anything or against anyone.

This is the message that true religion, philosophy, and psychology have proclaimed to embattled mankind throughout the ages. We must listen to this wisdom; otherwise, we remain in the jungle of despair.

And always, always, we must look within, for as the poet proclaims:

Truth is within ourselves . . .
There is an inmost center in us all,
Where Truth abides in fulness . . . and to know,
Rather consists in opening out a way
Whence the imprisoned splendor may escape . . .
                    Robert Browning, *Paracelsus*

The war is over for the man or woman who takes this not as mere poetry, but as a practical and inspiring guide to the peaceful life.

How to Escape Tension

In Chapter 5 we saw that all contacts between people are governed by definite psychological laws. One exceptionally important law is frequently overlooked or misunderstood. It is to your enrichment to grasp and apply it.

It is the law of compensation. Simply defined, it means that we get what we give. Give good; receive good. Give harm; get harm. Whether we are aware of this law or not, whether we believe in it or not, it still operates to our benefit or disadvantage. The wise man puts it on his side. The New Testament and other spiritual writings have much to say about this principle.

No modern authority makes it clearer than does Ralph Waldo Emerson in his classic essay, *Compensation:*

> *All infractions of love and equity in our social relations are speedily punished. They are punished by fear. Whilst I stand in simple relations to my fellow-man, I have no displeasure in meeting him. We meet as water meets water, or as two currents of air mix, with perfect diffusion and interpenetration of nature. But as soon as there is any departure from simplicity and attempt at halfness, or good for me that is not good for him, my neighbor feels the wrong; he shrinks from me as far as I have shrunk from him . . .*

It is a mistake to assume that our secret thoughts toward others do not matter. They matter very much. It is not sufficient to behave kindly toward people in public. Our secret manners, that is, our inner attitudes, must be just as kindly. Otherwise, we pay a painful price. If I think enviously toward another, I am punished on the spot for that envy. You can't be envious and happy at the same time. We must do more than *act* kindly; we must *be* kindly.

Always Learn From Your Experiences

Have you ever considered the difference between *knowledge* and *knowing?* As vital and as fascinating as it is, people fail to see the difference.

Knowledge is obtained from study, from books and lectures, from asking questions, and from attentive observation. But knowing is quite a different thing. It is the inward experiencing of acquired knowledge.

That is what we are after in this book. We want to know things by personal experience. That is what makes miracles happen to us.

> *Knowledge is the observation of a fact.*
> *Knowing is the inward experience of that fact.*

It is like a stranger, lost in a big city, who seeks to find the train station. A policeman tells him to go to Fourth Street, turn left, proceed two blocks, then turn right. The stranger now has the necessary knowledge, but by itself, it does nothing for him. He must turn that information into personal action, follow it through. He may even make mistakes as he proceeds, but so what? He is on his way. Finally, he arrives at the train station. He turns acquired knowledge into a rewarding inner experience. [MENTAL PICTURE 69]

Suppose I tell you that there is no need to be afraid of any other person on the face of the earth. Now, that is an absolute fact. It is the truth. But suppose that you are presently afraid of someone. Your present condition does not cancel that fact. It merely means that you must develop your understanding to where you prove it personally. So you must start with the knowledge that it is so, that no one on earth has power to frighten you. That is enough for now; start with just that much.

Then you must experiment with the fact. You must work at turning it into an actual experience. I assure you that you can do just this. Your growth might come through seeing that your timidity is merely an acquired state; it is not part of the essential

you. Or you might take inspiration from some other person who
has conquered his fears. There are dozens of helpful procedures.

OUTSTANDING IDEAS FROM THIS CHAPTER

1. Every individual can be free of fear and tension.
2. Fear departs as we dissolve the imaginary pictures we
   have about ourselves.
3. The True Self is entirely free of anxiety. Discover your
   True Self.
4. Work with the ideas of this chapter by following one
   clue at a time.
5. Give special attention to the plans offered for handling
   your future.
6. Release and relief come through self-understanding.
   Make self-knowledge your daily goal.
7. Declare your freedom from negative imagination.
8. Remember the two great truths supplied in this chapter.
9. The war against fear is won by the person who listens
   to the message of the True Self.
10. Turn your acquired knowledge into personal knowing.
    You will then experience that miracle of daily peace.

How to Enjoy Good
Health and Stay Young

Down in South America, there is a rare flower that requires rain inside its cup. The falling water revives and refreshes the entire plant. But the flower must be receptive to the rain. If it bends over too far, water cannot enter its cup. If the flower remains in a receptive position, its health is assured. [MENTAL PICTURE 70]

That short illustration is long on meaning. It spotlights one of the main pillars of robust, energetic living. The point is, we must be receptive to healthy ideas and impressions. Such ideas and truths come to us a thousand times a day, but unless we open our hearts and minds, they cannot enter with their supply of health and youthfulness.

For instance, Grace L. was not receptive to one of these health-giving truths. Her emptiness compelled her to sigh, "I'm always worn out. I know I'd feel better if I stopped running so hard. Why do I drain my strength in so many activities? I have a compulsive drive to get involved in this stupid activity or that mad chase. Why am I driven to get involved in so many pointless pursuits?"

"There is something you must understand, a new truth you must receive. You see, Grace, you really don't want to go *toward* these activities. You want to go *away* from something."

"You mean I want to escape from something?"

"Yes."

"What do I want to escape?"

"Yourself."

"My own self?"

"It is a self that you don't like, don't understand and don't trust; so it pains you. Your frantic activities are attempts to escape from an unwanted self. The objects of your chase really mean nothing to you. To prove this, notice how often you change directions. One day it's a new hobby, then a new club, then some social cause."

"That's right. I'm like a child wanting a new toy every day." She paused for a moment, then asked, "So I wear myself out with these pointless pursuits in an attempt to escape my own inner pain?"

"Yes. Try to see this clearly. Then, you will stop running. Your time and energy will then go into healthy channels, such as self-discovery. And you will no longer be tired."

How to Double Your Energy

Throughout this book we stress the need for *self*-awareness, *self*-insight, *self*-understanding. We emphasize the importance of becoming more conscious of ourselves. Why? Because no exercise is of more practical value.

I want to illustrate the practical value of self-awareness as it relates to your health and energy.

Suppose you are working frantically around the home or at the office. Your head whirls and your nerves strain. The pressure mounts almost unbearably. You are ready to explode.

What can you do? You can free yourself completely with the practical power of self-awareness.

Here is how:

Suddenly become aware that you *are* rushing, that you *are* under pressure, that you *are* jittery. This is quite a different state of awareness than you might imagine. It means that you actually *see yourself* in this nervous state. You become—for the first time that day—*conscious of your frantic state*. [MENTAL PICTURE 71]

Now, this awareness of your frantic state gives you power over it. You see, you cannot control a state that you are identified with, that is, a state you do not observe in yourself. But there is a calm self within you that can actually stand aside and observe another self, the frantic one. *This is self-awareness.* This is what gives you command.

Do you see the tremendous power here? Listen carefully: When you become aware of a frantic state you can then *see the difference* between a frantic state and a calm one. You see that there is an *alternative* to pressure. That alternative is calmness. When you are unaware of your pressure-state, you mistakenly think that it is the only state that exists. But now you are aware of the other way—calmness.

So catch yourself acting under pressure. Be deliberately aware of that tiresome state. Then, deliberately slow down. By an act of will, think and act and speak with voluntary leisure. This is something you can definitely do. And by doing so, you crack the frantic pattern.

Not only will you steadily establish a new pattern of unhurried work, but you will double your efficiency. You will get twice as much done in half the time. How come? Because your natural energies are no longer drained away in negative emotions. They are channeled constructively.

Never underestimate the practical power of self-awareness. Instead, prove it to yourself. You'll be glad you did.

Your Emotions and Your Health

Medical science has clearly demonstrated the effect of an individual's moods and emotions upon his health. Summed up, positive and cheery emotions build a supply of natural health, while negative and depressed moods cause psychosomatic illness. Let's connect this discovery with a Mental Picture:

You are seated in a theater, waiting for the movie to begin. The theater lights go off, and you settle back with an expectation of enjoyment. But as you watch the screen, you are confused. You react with discomfort at what you see. The screen is a jumble of vague figures and senseless movements. Suddenly, you realize what has happened. In some strange mix-up, two entirely different films are playing at the same time. They fight each other for space on the screen. No wonder nothing makes sense, no wonder you can't enjoy yourself!

But the man in the projection booth goes to work. He turns off the undesired film and leaves the wanted one running. Now, something interesting happens before your eyes. Gradually, the conflict fades away. The unwanted film grows dimmer and dimmer, while the right one becomes clearer. Finally, the screen is dominated by the correct film. The conflict disappears. Now you enjoy yourself! [MENTAL PICTURE 72]

That parallels the human situation. As long as a man has not found his True Self—the right film—he will be in conflict and contradiction. Nothing will satisfy him, nothing can cause more than a flash of pleasure, nothing will look right. No matter how hard he tries to find enduring enjoyment he will fail—and wonder why.

The reason why is that he is permitting needless negativities to play upon the screen of his mind. No wonder man cannot enjoy the performance.

But he can turn off the wrong film. He can permit the right one to dominate the screen of his consciousness. Then he is comfortable, relaxed, surrounded by a healthy atmosphere.

How does he replace the wrong film with the right one? How are negative feelings cut off?

Fifteen Tested Techniques

A review of various truths and techniques comes to our aid:

1. The power of self-awareness enables us to reject negative emotions the moment they try to sneak in.
2. *Self-knowledge aids you to see that unhappy moods are not a part of your True Self and therefore need not be endured.*
3. New attitudes create new feelings.

4. *We must have an emotionally charged desire to unlearn false ideas and to learn new truths.*

5. The emotion of love exists within us when we can be with other people without wanting something from them.

6. *Problems caused by negative emotions, such as headaches, nervousness, and insomnia, disappear from the life of whoever comes into harmony with natural life-principles.*

7. Your values change as you develop inwardly. You then laugh at things that formerly pained you.

8. *As a man really sees how much health and energy he wastes in worry, envy, disappointment, and other useless emotions, he stops them.*

9. The great secret of youthful living is to enjoy the *self*, not material possessions!

10. *Heartache and suffering decrease to the extent that we see the fact about something without adding our personal opinion to that fact.*

11. You are starting the right way to dissolve negative emotions by honestly seeing that they are there.

12. *When your mind is really free, there are no emotional prisons whatsoever to think about. A man free of prison has no need to think of either freedom or imprisonment.*

13. You loosen the pain of a negative feeling by refusing to identify with it; that is, by not seeing it as a permanent part of you, but rather as a feeling that merely passes through you.

14. *When you recover your True Self you are no longer in conflict over what you want or what you should do. Your True Self always knows just what to do and what not to do.*

15. Your persistent pursuit of the principles of Truth will certainly produce inner change, which, in turn, produces warm feelings of well-being.

Come to Life!

Imagine yourself standing before an impressive painting by one of the great artists. It has a colorful background and interesting people in the foreground. Now, imagine the picture suddenly coming to life. The people walk and gesture, the trees sway in the wind. It creates an entirely different impression, doesn't it? [MENTAL PICTURE 73]

That is what the truth should do for you. As you read and reflect, it should come alive within your mind. This is what happens when you read with a welcoming attitude, for instance, an idea that was more or less motionless; it now moves upward into your active understanding. You may have previously seen only words on a page; you now experience life-liberating truth. An idea passes from outward observation to inward awareness. *It changes you.*

Remember this: The truth, when it arrives, is always different from what we thought it would be. If we imagine that we already know the truth, that imagination is based on old and habitual ideas. But the truth is always something entirely new to the mind; therefore, we cannot possibly imagine it. Just as we cannot know what a new day is like before we experience it, we cannot think accurately about a new truth until we first live it. *"Do not require a description of the countries towards which you sail. The description does not describe them to you, and to-morrow you arrive there and know them by inhabiting them."* (Emerson— *The Over-Soul*) As we dare to drop our conditioned opinions, we make room for the truth.

Let's take the truth that you can be entirely free of your past. To most people, this is a desired state but not an experienced one. It *can* be experienced by anyone who comes alive to the truth about it.

"I can believe," an inquirer said, "that the principles you speak about can change my future, but how can they change my foolish past? What has happened, has happened. How can I alter it?"

You can alter your mental and emotion reaction to it. That is the entire secret. The events remain the same, but your thinking toward them is transformed so that they no longer bother you. You break the connection, just as you'd break a pipe bringing impure water into your home.

See *yourself* differently. You are still calling yourself by your old labels, such as being cruel, arrogant, or whatever you used to be. You are still identifying yourself as these states. When you see your new self, your True Self, your viewpoint changes. This is not easy to explain in words; it must be experienced.

You are like a man who crosses a stormy river in a rowboat and continues to carry the boat on his back. The river is crossed, but you don't see it as yet. In your past, you were hypnotized by the evil magician of illusion. In that hypnotized state you did self-defeating things. But you can now wake up. Then you will see that you did those things while in a hypnotized state. But now you are no longer hypnotized. You are awake. When you are no longer hypnotized, when you awake to your True Self, you no longer hate yourself for anything you did in the past—anything at all.

It makes an enormous difference. Here is something else to remember. An inability to detach yourself from the past is a cause of present mistakes—often the very same mistakes. Your emotional tie with the past destroys your present good judgment. So freedom from the hypnotized self automatically prevents you from repeating the old and harmful living patterns. Your True Self finds a new line of action, a sensible and self-advancing one. Work with all this.

How to Keep Your Youthful Feelings

Do you sometimes catch a fleeting glimpse of how you used to feel when you were younger? It's such a wonderful feeling of freedom. Is it right to yearn for these younger days when life seemed so carefree?

It is not the younger time period for which you yearn; it is the state of inner liberty that you want. You had this happy state in past days, but adult confusions and desires stole it from you.

It can be regained and retained. Such flashes of freedom come in unexpected moments, usually when you are thinking of something else. But this brief glimpse is perfect evidence that the happy state is still there; as a matter of fact, it is always there. It is like catching a glimpse of a beautiful lake as you travel swiftly between two hills. It is only a glance, but it proves the lake is there. The glimpse may vanish temporarily, but that need not bother you. With right action you can live in a cheerful and carefree state twenty-four hours a day.

No one has expressed all this with more beauty and clarity than Henry David Thoreau in *Walden:*

Sham and delusions are esteemed for soundest truths, while reality is fabulous. If men would steadily observe realities only, and not allow themselves to be deluded, life,

*to compare it with such things as we know, would be like
a fairy tale and the Arabian Nights' Entertainments. If we
respected only what is inevitable and has a right to be,
music and poetry would resound along the streets. When
we are unhurried and wise, we perceive that only great and
worthy things have any permanent and absolute existence,
that petty fears and petty pleasures are but the shadow of
reality. This is always exhilarating and sublime. By clos-
ing the eyes and slumbering, and consenting to be deceived
by shows, men establish and confirm their daily life of
routine and habit everywhere, which still is built on purely
illusory foundations. Children, who play life, discern its
true law . . .*

How to Stop Worrying About Living and Start to Live

Suppose you were standing at the rail of a great ocean liner,
alongside the captain, and witnessed the following scene:

The captain notices a man adrift on a flimsy raft a short
distance from the ship. The captain calls for him to come as
close as possible in order to make the rescue. But the man
stands there and argues with the captain. He asks whether
the ship is safe to board, whether the captain knows his business and how long before the ship reaches port. He does everything but come aboard. [MENTAL PICTURE 74]

You would think it incredible. What man in desperate need
of rescue would behave like that? You would want to yell out,
"Man, get to the point!"

It is really unfortunate how so many people fail to get to the
point in their lives.

The point of every man's life is to be content. Not busy, not
demanding, not arguing, but to simply be content.

Man's great mistake is to think that he must work at contentment. Don't work at living—live.

"Always run to the short way," wrote Roman emperor and
philosopher Marcus Aurelius, "and the short way is the natural."

People try to place their contentment outside themselves. That
is like thinking that the sparkle is outside the diamond.

Do not try to be content with *something*. If you do, you will be
anxious that that something will sooner or later fail you. Do not
be content with *something*. Just be content. Do not seek a reason

for it. True contentment needs no object outside itself. It simply *is*.

You cannot *try* to be content. But you can *be* content. Right where you are. Right now. Without first adding something. Without first thinking about it.

Thinking about contentment offers no supply—any more than thinking about an apple satisfies your hunger.

As a rule, people do not penetrate all the way to the truth of this idea of effortless peace. You can be the exception to the rule.

You can get to the point of your life.

The point is to be your True Self. The True Self is contentment itself.

How to End Suffering and Pain

I want to give you an idea that I sincerely hope will startle you.

If it does, you can use it to escape steadfastly from all kinds of inner pain.

The idea is simple, yet of far greater significance than you may first suspect. Here it is:

See the difference between *relief* from inner suffering and the *ending* of suffering. It is quite possible for mental and emotional pain to come to a happy ending. Even if you cannot presently grasp this as a fact, I assure you that it is so.

Also, of course, the conquest of emotional pain naturally refreshes your physical self with new health and energy. Medical science declares this a certainty.

Let's take an example of the difference between temporary relief and permanent freedom. Suppose you frequently get lonely. You use all sorts of things to cover it up, like social activities and hobbies. But still it remains. So you decide to get rid of it for all time. So you investigate loneliness itself and discover that it stems from lack of insight into your genuine nature. Then, by finding your True Self, you are never again lonely, for the True Self *cannot experience* that sad state.

Get temporary relief, if necessary, but also plan a long-range program for discarding pain altogether.

What clear-thinking person takes a pain-easing pill every hour when a far superior medicine can banish the very source of pain?

What is this superior medicine? You will be pleased to hear:

It is the truths and principles you have been absorbing all along in these pages. They have already shined their healthy rays upon you.

Everything you have sincerely received has already helped you, and will continue to do so. Just as plant roots on a hillside hold rainwater, so does your mind catch and store these energetic truths. So, review them often. They are good medicine.

Summary: No longer seek mere relief from pain. Seek its absolute ending. It is yours for the seeking.

How to Smile at Things That Once Made You Ill

Use this Mental Picture:

Imagine yourself speeding down the highway toward the dry desert. As you travel along, the weather gets uncomfortably warm, and the scenery becomes dull. You decide that you don't like it; you are tired of traveling toward unpleasant country. So you make up your mind to change your direction, to reverse yourself and head for the mountains at your back.

But, of course, you cannot come to a sudden stop. Even though you make the decision, your momentum carries you forward for awhile. But you slow down, come to a stop, turn around and start off in the opposite direction. Slowly but surely you gather speed as you head toward the mountains.

Now you begin to feel different, both physically and emotionally. The change in direction performs the miracle of change in feeling. You actually experience the cooler air; you respond with pleasure to the lovelier scenery.

Now that you personally feel the difference in the two courses, nothing can ever persuade you to abandon your new direction. By your own observation and feeling, you know that there is a difference. You also know that as you continue in this right direction, you will feel *increasingly* good. Everything will be much better, including your health. [MENTAL PICTURE 75]

That is a good picture of what happens to the person who has caught his Magnificent Glimpse of the new life. As a man honestly faces the fact of his dry destination, he immediately feels the desire to change directions. And he can do so!

Remember, your objective is to arrive at the point where you can *see definite change in your inner self*. This requires strict self-honesty, for the human mind is tricky. A good feeling caused by something outside of you is not self-change. Self-change is *self*-change; it is caused by the gradual appearance of your True Self within you. You may feel good over a compliment, but that is not self-change, any more than a short charge of electricity changes an electric motor. It merely spins it briefly. If you depend on other people to make you feel good, you will feel anxious. Depend upon your True Self, and you are anxious over nothing.

What are some of these changes that make us healthier and happier? What good things appear to us once we change direction? Let's see.

Watch how you smile at things that used to make you feel ill. You previously thought that by losing your friend or your job, your prestige or your reputation, your companion, counselor, social group, your spouse or lover or sex partner, your power, honor, money, youthfulness, success—you previously thought that the loss of these things meant that *you* were lost.

Now you are wiser. Now you do not identify with these things. You do not take them as *you*, the real you. You have separated your acquisitions from your true identity. You no longer imagine yourself to be anyone; you *know* who you really are.

You can smile. For the first time you see something utterly fantastic. You see that any so-called loss is no loss at all. Not *really*. You see that you never really owned these things in the first place; you merely identified with them; you mistakenly took them as part of you. But you no longer take the loss of these acquired things as a loss to *you*. No, because you are someone entirely different. You are your True Self. Now you are glad to lose whatever belongs to the False Self, such as pride and pretense, because you see how painful they are to you.

Now you are wiser. You now see that you cannot lose anything because, psychologically speaking, you never really owned anything. When you have nothing, you have nothing to lose. Now you draw a deep breath, perhaps for the first time in your life. What a strange but wonderful situation. You own nothing, and yet you own everything!

I am not writing this with any intention of being mystical or mysterious. I am telling you about a practical miracle.

Dr. Paul Brunton describes this kingly state:

There is, however, such a condition as coming into tune with the Infinite, which you can always rely upon as producing an inner sense of utter satisfaction, of lacking nothing, of perfect contentment . . . How restful and how happy to be free from the torments of desire! Just to abide in quietude! No matter where you are, to be free of restless desires, to be ever at ease! Here is a calm that is unbroken and eternal, and not dependent upon the state of your finances or on the state of the world peace, but only on the eternal reality which is ever-present within yourself. This is true peace. The desire for constant excitement disappears from a man into whom the quietude of the soul has entered.[1]

How to End Nervousness

You see, when you uncover your True Self—which you have had all along, whether you knew it or not—that is all you need. This is so, even though you do not presently understand it. It is simply so. The existence of Reality does not depend upon our acceptance of it any more than the existence of Niagara Falls depends upon our seeing it.

When you follow the principles set down in these pages you change direction. This new direction gradually but definitely verifies itself. You begin to see things that you never before suspected of having existence. You are both surprised and delighted. When you see the practical benefits of self-change, you will exclaim, "What a wonderful difference it makes! Why didn't I see it long ago? Well, no matter; I am now traveling in the right direction. I'm on my way. All is well."

You will no longer be nervous. You will not be shocked by exterior events. Because your emotions are now guided by a higher form of intelligence, they no longer have you at their mercy. *You are in charge of the way you want to feel.* Emotions perform healthy functions only.

This is really quite an adventure. You are no longer jittery at being by yourself or at meeting strangers or at confronting an unexpected happening.

What is the real cause of nervousness?

The clinging to a false sense of identity. You are jittery because

---

[1] Paul Brunton, *Discover Yourself* (New York: E. P. Dutton and Co., Inc., 1939).

you are not really the person you pretend to be. For example, suppose that you insistently pretend that you know all the answers to your problems. You will then be nervous over self-exposure.

How do we destroy these unhealthy pretenses?

Be exactly who and what you are without shame or guilt or apology. Hide nothing from yourself. Bravely look at all your pretenses and see them as pretenses. You need not tell others, but expose yourself to yourself. Self-honesty, though painful at the time, is like sunshine dissolving fog. As the fog clears, you recognize your True Self—which is never nervous over anything.

How can we start working on this healthy idea?

Start to suspect that there is an entirely new way to live your daily life. I assure you that there is.

HEALTHY PLANS TO REMEMBER

1. Be receptive to healthy ideas and techniques.
2. Unhealthy thoughts and damaging emotions are destroyed by becoming aware of them.
3. Remember the fifteen tested techniques in this chapter.
4. You can be totally free of painful feelings connected with the past. And this freedom refreshes everything today.
5. The sensible point in life is to dwell in healthy contentment.
6. Seek absolute ending of inner pain, not temporary relief.
7. The guaranteed way to be vigorous and youthful is to first change the inner self. Energy follows.
8. You are quite capable of reacting in a happy and healthy manner to everything that happens to you.
9. When you find your True Self, nervousness vanishes forever.
10. Suspect that there is a new and enchanted world for your discovery. There really is.

13

How to Put More Life and Love in Your Living

Think of happiness as a state of *inner liberty*. That is exactly what it is. It is never anything else. It will help if you forget the word *happiness* altogether. Substitute the term *inner liberty*. It works favorably upon your thinking habits. It connects inner liberty with the genuine meaning of happiness. And that puts you on the right track.

It is not excitement or a feeling of sensation. Excitement always has an opposite; sooner or later the pendulum swings back to boredom or depression. Excitement depends upon an emotional attachment to something, perhaps a new home or a compliment. Inwardly, you may attach yourself to a daydream or a hope of getting rich. But these excitements have no stability; they wear off. So you are kept in a nervous search for more excitement, which exhausts you. But when you find inner liberty you are free from anxious dependence upon contrived thrills. Then you are happy. You are happy whether or not you get the new home, or whether or not your daydream comes true.

Personal progress can be likened to a railroad train that stops periodically to drop some passengers and to pick up new ones. We must regularly drop our false ideas while picking up new concepts. Drop the notion that you must fight life; pick up the truth that the war is over. Drop the myth that past mistakes have a hold on you today; pick up the fact that every new day is new. [MENTAL PICTURE 76]

How to Mine the Diamonds of Happiness

No subject of human interest is more talked about and less understood than that of happiness. People want to know:

Does happiness really exist?
Why haven't I found it?
What obstacles stand in my way?
Why is the search so confusing?
How can I attain happiness?

I will give you an avenue of approach that leads to inner quietness. You must, however, persist in your effort to understand all that is presented. You must not resist something simply because it seems contrary to your present ideas. Please explore with me with a receptive state of mind. That is how to understand the truth about happiness.

The discovery of a noted diamond field supplies a good illustration for our point: A South African adventurer was convinced that diamonds could be found in a certain section of the countryside. But it was a vast area. Its physical features included a thick forest, a high plateau, a prairie, grassy plains, and remote valleys. At first, it seemed like an impossible task; there were just too many places to explore. But his intelligent reasoning came up with a simple and effective program: He eliminated all areas where diamonds could *not* be found. For instance, he knew that certain valleys did not meet the test of probabilities. So, by knowing where diamonds were *not*, he was left with the single area where they *were*. The diamonds were easily located at the entrance of a valley. [MENTAL PICTURE 77]

The truth about that diamond field parallels the truth about happiness. Just as those diamonds were *already there*, ready for the persistent explorer, so is your happiness *already within you,* ready for your discovery.

Do not try to "find happiness." It is the wrong approach. Here is where practically everyone makes their big mistake. Rather, eliminate those areas where happiness *cannot* be found—and deep down within himself every man knows where it cannot be found. Peace cannot be located by anyone who insists that his illusions are realities. Nor can it be located by the person who hides his despair behind frantic activities. It is never found by the man who believes merely what he wants to believe. By eliminating these worthless areas, this diamonds of happiness are finally found.

Using Your True Self to Gain Beauty and Contentment

I want to tell you of something of utmost importance to every department of your daily life. It can charge you with fresh energy, develop your mental forces and make you happy. However, before I tell you about it, I want you to place yourself into an open frame of mind, to be freely receptive to the message. After all, the manner in which we listen to something has everything to do with results. By losing ourselves in the beauty of a symphony, it becomes a part of us. That is what you should do with this message—permit it to become a part of your innermost being.

In an attitude of attentive receptivity, then, I want to give you some words of enormous encouragement:

Failure is absolutely impossible to the man or woman who sincerely and persistently searches for his abundantly wealthy True Self.

Please reflect upon this for a moment before reading on. The patiently persistent person eventually makes a delightful discovery. He finds that everything that happens to him can be used for self-advancement. How can this be? Because every event, happy or sad, supplies an opportunity for putting the True Self to the test, letting it prove itself. It is always our *reaction* to an event that counts, not the event itself.

You can learn to always react correctly, dynamically, cheerfully. How the veil of misunderstanding bursts apart before the man who sees this!

Here is how Dr. Raynor C. Johnson expresses the same bright truth:

> Each circumstance and event, tragic or happy, is attracted to us by what we have been and are, and in itself offers to us, by a right reaction to it, the opportunity of spiritual development.[1]

The truth that frees us into health and happiness might be likened to a beautiful woman with a dozen ardent suitors. She asks, "Do you love me above all else, or are you merely seeking a new thrill?" Or, "Will you be faithful to me in spite of temptations?" Or, "Do you want me for myself, or merely to prove how persuasive you are?"

The man who gives the right answers will hear the truth respond. She never fails the man who pursues her with ardent sincerity and affection. When he places her before all else, she willingly comes to him. [MENTAL PICTURE 78]

How to Predict Your Future Fortune

What brightness would illuminate your day if you knew that your future holds good fortune! It would light up your face and add spring to your step. I assure you that this brightness can be yours. Fear of future misfortune lurks in a corner of the mind of man, draining body and spirit. But it need not be so.

You can accurately predict future fortune for yourself—and make it come true. Many men and women have already done so by reading my previous book, *SECRETS OF MENTAL MAGIC: How to Use Your Full Power of Mind*. Chapter 6, entitled *Mental Magic Predicts Your Future*, supplies full details for becoming a prophet of prosperity. In this section I want to share some highlights with you:

"I feel that future circumstances may be too much for me."

You create your own future circumstances. Change yourself today and tomorrow's circumstances will be what you want.

"I don't understand the need for self-transformation."

Trying to enrich tomorrow without first enriching yourself is

---

[1] Raynor C. Johnson, *The Imprisoned Splendour* (New York: Harper and Row, Publishers, Incorporated, 1953).

like trying to hit a target with an empty rifle. Your True Self is your ammunition.

"How do I know that these ideas about self-change are really accurate?"

Test them. One way is to see that you repeat the same unhappy experiences day after day because you *don't* change yourself.

"What kind of friends will I have in the future?"

Those on your own psychological level. Like attracts like. If you want loftier friends, raise your level of being.

"Does this inner alteration affect material things, like my business and finances?"

It affects everything. If you change positions to face east instead of west you see and react differently to everything out there.

"Does the law of cause and effect enter into our future?"

Absolutely. Do something today and you get a result tomorrow.

"How can I start changing myself and forthcoming days?"

Work patiently with the principles of Psycho-Pictography. They insure your future fortune.

How to Know Always What's Best for You

The question came, "I realize that happiness depends largely upon the daily decisions we make, but I find it hard to decide what is good for me. I don't know how to serve my best interests. Is there some simple rule I can follow?"

There is a very simple and extremely practical rule. If you will apply it to everything that you do and feel and think, you will more and more see what is best for you. And that results in a richer life.

The rule is: *If it really contributes to your best interest, it is right.*

The other side of the same rule is: *If it hinders your self-development, it is wrong.*

Get the habit of mentally sorting things out as they come along. In Washington's fruit factories the apples are carried down an assembly line to be sorted according to quality. Think of your day's events in that way. Stand at the assembly line to check and choose. It is perfectly within your power to select the right and reject the wrong. Ask yourself, "Is this way of thinking a benefit or a harm?" And, "Is this action a help or a hindrance to my over-all self-development?" [MENTAL PICTURE 79]

This sorting process builds a clear awareness of what your best-interests really are. You can easily tell which thoughts and actions are profitable and which are a loss. It is a richly rewarding process, this process of *choosing in favor of yourself!*

Your physical well-being is certain to improve as you apply this principle. Say, for example, that you catch negative imaginations running through your mind. You can wisely reason like this: "Negative imaginations are harmful in every way. They drain my strength, make me nervous; they disturb my sleep and hinder happiness and zest. Why should I permit these harmful thoughts to run loose in my mind? I shouldn't. I have power to refuse them. That is exactly what I do—right now."

Can you think of anything more healthy than choosing in favor of yourself?

How to Know You're Getting Somewhere in Life

One of the most frequently asked questions from those who want to get somewhere with their lives is this:

"How can I get what I want?"

This is an essential question. The how-to-do-it is of paramount importance to your attainment. If the method is right, results will be right. We find gold by searching the earth. We find beauty by searching the sky. We must look in the right places to find whatever we want. Anyone can learn to look in the right places.

I want to give you a workable method for achieving your aims, whatever they may be. It consists of *not* doing what you usually do. Instead of doing something, you *stop* doing something. When you cease a wrong action, you make way for a workable one. Work with these examples:

Stop trying to be happy. Try to understand the causes of unhappiness.
Stop thinking you must change conditions before you change yourself. Change yourself, and you will naturally change your conditions.

Stop despairing over what you cannot do at present. Whole-heartedly do whatever you can at present.

Stop feeling that life is pointless. Use the principles of truth to discover the point of life.

Stop falling victim to negative emotions. Realize that they have absolutely no power over you.

Stop anxiously fighting all the complications in your life. Simplify your affairs.

Stop feeling useless guilt. Try to discover the reasons for a false sense of guilt.

Stop being so concerned with social popularity. Work at self-acceptance.

Stop your frantic search for answers. Be quietly receptive to your True Self which knows the right answers.

Thomas Jefferson said, "It is better to have no ideas than false ones." Stop employing unworkable ideas and methods. Leave a vacuum. Watch it fill with bright ideas!

Suppose you were told about a fabulously rich city, lost for centuries in the jungles of some remote region of the world. Further suppose that you wanted to find it. You wouldn't frantically rush out the front door and head toward it. No, you would understand that you must put first things first. You would collect maps, study the region, prepare equipment. Having put first things first, you guarantee your success. [MENTAL PICTURE 80]

We must put first things first in our search for happiness. The first thing is to understand what it is all about, to separate fact from myth.

One of our first understandings is that happiness appears when the inner self is in harmony with external realities.

We start by changing our inner attitudes and beliefs, not by trying to alter outer conditions. A man's chief problem is his persistently wrong assumption that happiness comes from changing his exterior conditions. As if we change anything in ourselves merely by putting on another coat! We mistakenly think that if this circumstance or that person would change we would be different. But we wouldn't. It never really occurs to us that we have followed this false course over the years and it never leads anywhere. We are constantly surprised that we get nowhere, yet we keep running.

When we possess inner harmony *it is the very same thing as external harmony*. What a great change takes place in a man's life when he sees this as a practical truth.

It really doesn't make any difference whether other people appreciate us or not. But in our self-centered attitudes we think that it does—and so we are unhappy. We really have no problem when some plan of ours doesn't turn out as we wanted. The problem arises only when we identify ourselves as victims of injustice.

Whenever some unexpected event bothers you, tell yourself, "It makes a difference only if I think it does—and I don't think it does." This is not helpless submission. It is understanding— and genuine happiness.

How to Fill Each Day with Delightful Surprises

As you persistently work with Mental Pictures you meet many delightful surprises along the way. This is a good place to introduce one of them.

You remember in Chapter 1 the Mental Picture about the man and his castle. We said that if he were to venture forward just a step or two, if he would dare to leave his old and familiar mental grounds, he would glimpse something new. Now, let's suppose that you decide to venture forward, that you are tired of the old ways and wish to discover your higher world. So you take your first steps forward, that is, you begin to abandon the False Self with all its boring habits, rigid beliefs, and pointless actions.

Now, you sight the corner of the castle, you catch a tiny glimpse of another way to think and act. Remember, *you will be surprised at seeing it*. It will be entirely different from what you had expected to see. Why is this? Because you stepped forward with a preconceived idea of what you would and should see. You might say that you had built a mental frame which you expected the picture to fit. But it doesn't. In no way does the preconceived idea match the new reality you encounter. And so you are surprised.

But after the surprise comes the delight. You realize that here is something entirely new. It is not merely the reworking of the old idea. It is not an exchange of one worthless belief for another.

It is not the dropping of an old coat for another worn one. It is an entirely new garment, one you had neither seen nor worn before!

When you reach this stage where you are first surprised and then delighted, *you know that you are on the right path at last.* Yes, there may still be considerable confusion and doubt, but you have gained an inner light that can never be extinguished. It is there and you know it. Now, your excitement grows. Having glimpsed that one tiny corner of the castle, you can hardly wait to see more of it.

The question may arise, "Is this what you call a mystical experience?" The answer is a definite *yes,* but something should be added: Any experience you have—whether you call it a mystical event, a growth in mental maturity, or deeper self-insight—is a genuine experience only if *it changes your actions in everyday life.* This is the whole purpose of such experiences—to put you more at ease with others and with yourself, to increase home harmony, to enable you to meet challenges calmly and constructively. The supreme test is: If it is real, it is practical. If it changes things for the better, you can call it anything you like, but you are in contact with a new and vital force—your True Self.

Dr. Edwin A. Burtt supplies an inspiring description of the insight of the True Self:

> . . . *you find that instead of becoming weak, crushed, empty (as might have been expected) you gain a new strength and wholeness which you realize is the only real strength and wholeness. You achieve a knowledge that is the only real knowledge, a freedom and happiness that alone truly deserves these names. By non-action—that is, by abandoning the aggressive self-assertion that alone seems effective action to others—you find that in reality you are accomplishing all the ends that are worth accomplishing.*[2]

Then, when all this happens, we are in love. Then, we are surprised to find that love is something entirely different from what we thought it was. It makes us see everything in a new way; it enables us to be inwardly peaceful whenever we are unjustly

---

[2] Edwin A. Burtt, *Man Seeks the Divine* (New York: Harper and Row, Publishers, Incorporated, 1957).

attacked by others, it takes away the hounding desires that formerly kept us anxious and frustrated.

Augustine, the religious wise man, once supplied a famous answer to the problems of life, saying, "Love, and do what you like."

If we really love, we can do what we like, for then we will harm neither others nor ourselves. Genuine love can never do harm in any way.

What is love? Love is first a state of being and *then* an outer action. Love is first of all what you inwardly *are*, and secondly, what you *do*. It must come in this order, otherwise, it is not love but something masquerading as love.

To the degree that we are genuinely loving, to that same degree are we genuinely happy.

Are You Fighting Dragons?

I want to discuss with you a magnificent truth that runs like a golden thread through all the great religious and philosophical teachings. When firmly grasped, it delivers permanent happiness into your hands.

It is the truth of *non-resistance*.

Whenever we resist something—perhaps an unkind remark, a shocking event, or a depressing feeling—our very resistance indicates a belief in the power of that event to hurt us. Although it is really powerless, our mistaken belief in it induces despair.

But by not resisting, we dissolve the false belief and consequently the false power for harm.

Think this through.

When we no longer resist the event, we no longer believe in its false power. When we no longer believe in its false power, we no longer suffer. The suffering is in our acceptance of its false power, not in the event itself.

There is really nothing to fear, therefore, nothing to resist. No one can hurt you, no matter what they do to you. Nothing can upset you, regardless of what happens to you. It is not the outer action that brings unhappiness; it is the inner reaction that causes pain. Such a simple truth, when deeply understood, creates miraculous inner tranquility.

No, we need not fight, we need not resist. *We need only to understand.*

A man caught up in the illusion that anyone has power to hurt him is like a knight who believes in the myth of dreadful dragons. Believing in them the knight enters the dark woods with drawn sword, expecting a battle. Every shadow then becomes a fierce dragon that he must slay. Then, as the light dawns, he sees that it was his acceptance of the myth that made him fight so anxiously and so unnecessarily. Understanding this, he lowers his sword and rides peacefully onward. [MENTAL PICTURE 81]

Take a man battling for a satisfying purpose in life. For a while he struggles for power or popularity. When the reaction of futility comes from such a battle, as it always does, he falls into despondency. Next, he seeks a purpose by getting involved in a variety of social, religious, or money-making activities. But he is battling for nothing; for involvement in any exterior activity sooner or later ends with a terrifying sense of futility.

Once that man ceases to fight for a purpose, as he becomes quiet, he finds the genuine purpose of life—which is the inward experiencing of the Truth itself. Then and then only will his outward activities make sense. And then, whatever they may be, rich or poor, famous or unknown, he has no anxiety toward them whatever. Having the Truth, he has all things.

Now You Can Use What the Great Teachers Knew and Used

You must not take this as an airy philosophy having nothing to do with everyday living. It is the only thing that gives real meaning to everyday existence. A man once said to me, "Your ideas are very appealing but I wish I could see their practical application." I told him, "Ask yourself whether you are *now* leading a practical life? Is it practical to be afraid at every corner? If you are ruthlessly honest you will see how impractical a life you now lead. The alternative is before you. Take it."

I know very well the difficulty of starting your program of non-resistance. I know how the mind's entrenched habits and ego-defenses will scream in protest. But a man need only see that his peace is at stake. Then he will choose to ally himself with this liberating principle.

You can start this very moment. You can begin clearing the woods of illusionary dragons with the calm intention, "From this moment on I withdraw all false beliefs that this situation has power to harm me. Because I understand that resistance implies belief, I no longer resist. Why should I resist a non-existent dragon?"

In his classic book, *Cosmic Consciousness* (E. P. Dutton & Co., Inc.), Dr. Richard Maurice Bucke points out that all the great spiritual giants of history possessed a common characteristic: They understood the friendliness of the universe; from their lofty level of consciousness they saw nothing to fight, only an illusion to see through. Among these enlightened individuals were Christ, Buddha, Socrates, Benedict Spinoza, Walt Whitman, Alfred Tennyson.

Watch the energy with which your world changes before your eyes as you cease to resist. To whom does this energy come? "This energy does not descend into individual life on any other condition than entire possession. It comes to the lowly and simple; it comes to whomsoever will put off what is foreign and proud; it comes as insight; it comes as serenity and grandeur. When we see those whom it inhabits, we are apprised of new degrees of greatness. From that inspiration the man comes back with a changed tone." (Emerson, *The Over-Soul*)

A seed changes miraculously into a colorful rose because it offers no resistance to higher powers. It gladly surrenders to the warm earth and cheery sunshine—and grows as intended. And so can we surrender the False Staff to higher powers—and grow as intended. [MENTAL PICTURE 82]

Resist not. Have the courage and the wisdom not to resist. You will find yourself above the world of strife. This is exactly where you will be, even if you do not presently see how it can be so. Try it. Then you will see.

FOR YOUR BRIGHTER DAYS

1. Think of happiness as a state of inner liberty.
2. Happiness comes easily and naturally as we drop our false concepts about life.
3. Remember the Mental Picture of the beautiful woman. It contains a rich lesson.
4. By working with the principles of Psycho-Pictography, you learn to predict your future fortunes.
5. Right action consists in choosing in favor of your true interests.
6. Stop self-defeating actions. Then, right actions are revealed to you.
7. The first step toward greater happiness is to investigate happiness itself.
8. Love and happiness go hand in hand.
9. Practice non-resistance. Nothing will do more for you.
10. You ascend as intended into loftier living as you become receptive to higher powers.

14

How to Avoid Mistakes and Solve Problems

Suppose you were a gardening expert and a neighbor told you, "I have a problem with my apple tree. It doesn't yield fruit. No matter how carefully I cultivate it, year after year, no apples appear. So I want to ask your advice: In order to make it fruitful, should I move it to the north part of my yard or to the south?"

You would reply, "You must understand something. It won't make the slightest difference whether you move it north, south, east or west; it still won't bear apples. The basic problem is the tree's incapacity to bear fruit. You don't change its capacity by moving its position. If you want apples, get an entirely new tree, one capable of supplying fruit." [MENTAL PICTURE 83]

No one really solves his problems by changing his occupation or his spouse or his residence or anything else exterior to himself. He must exchange his False Self for his True Self. Then he won't need to solve problems—they will be non-existent. I am not exaggerating and I am not writing this merely to make you feel good. I am saying that your problems will cease to exist. The True Self—you can call it the Kingdom of Heaven within, if you prefer —has no problems whatsoever. This is something you can prove for yourself. Then you will have solved the great mystery of life.

"If I am capable of clearing myself," you may ask, "how come I fail so often?"

"Because you are trying to do the impossible."

"In what way?"

"By trying to perform above your present level of understanding. The *Mona Lisa* was painted out of the high artistic level of Leonardo da Vinci. *Finlandia* was composed from the creative heights of Jean Sibelius. Likewise, psychologically, you must *understand* before you can *do*."

You cannot get rid of a sense of futility by using your usual thoughts. Employing your conditioned mind is like blundering around in a roomful of distorting mirrors, the kind you see at amusement parks You must ascend to a new level, that of *awareness,* of *increased consciousness*. Where awareness is, there are no distorting mirrors. You can see for yourself that this is so. Apply the principles of Psycho-Pictography.

How Dissolving Problems Is Easier Than Solving Them

A troubled person will react in one of three ways to a psychological truth that could free him:

1. He will accept and work with it. He may do so with some timidity, but he courageously goes ahead. Such a man has attained a level of understanding where he sees something of value. He sees that the sacrifice of his fixed and egotistical ideas and the acceptance of new and workable concepts is necessary for his happiness.

2. He will resentfully reject it. His False Self recognizes the truth as a threat to its existence. All the falsehoods and illusions of the False Self will resist furiously. Such a person dimly realizes that he is acting against his own best interests, but at this stage of awareness, he is unable to do anything about it.

3. He will act with seeming indifference, although this indifference is another form of rejection. When such a man meets a truth

that could help him, his indifference becomes a thin mask to hide his fear of something new and different.

The first man cannot fail to find a problem-free life. His success is assured by his willingness to give up the False Self, which is the cause of *all* problems and pains.

A man came to me to complain that other people didn't behave correctly toward him. People were inconsiderate, they didn't keep their word, they took advantage of his good nature, and so on. I asked him, "Why do you demand that others behave the way *you* prefer? The truth is, people always behave the way they are, not according to your wishes. Do you see that the problem lies in your unrealistic expectations?"

That man did a very intelligent thing. He went to work on his own mental demands toward people. Instead of trying to change their behavior, he altered his viewpoints about their behavior. He simply let people behave as they wished, without wanting or expecting them to be any different. In that healthy state he found peace.

That is a good example of how a receptive attitude toward a psychological truth can solve a problem by dissolving its very cause. Where can you receive fresh insight that will dissolve a problem?

How to Conceive a Cheering Mental Picture

Let me give you an encouraging Mental Picture:

Suppose you want to paint the walls of your two-story home, starting with the first floor. You make a telephone call, and the truck from the hardware store rolls up with several buckets of paint. Although you are not ready for the paint intended for the second floor, you want to keep it in a convenient place, so you carry the buckets upstairs and leave them. You then descend and paint the first floor. When that is finished to your satisfaction, you go upstairs where the paint you now need is waiting for you. It was there all the time, of course, but now that you are ready for it, it is ready for you. [MENTAL PICTURE 84]

The same with truthful ideas. Don't try to use all of them at once. You can do only so much work at one time. Concentrate on the first floor of understanding. Be receptive to the more advanced ideas of the second story, but don't worry over them. Set them some place upstairs in your mind and ignore them. Put first things first. Take my word for it, when you are ready for higher truth, it will be ready for you. Remember, it is absolutely impossible to lose a truthful idea once you have seen it, even if it was only a brief flash of insight. Sooner or later, when you have finished your work on the first floor, the material you need on the upper level will be right there. And you will know exactly how to apply it to make your life more comfortable and more colorful.

How Not to Solve a Problem

One of the best procedures for clearing confusion is to see plainly what does *not* work.

One course that has never worked and never will work is *distraction*. A distraction is anything that prevents us from looking the problem in the face with a mind made up to locate the answer.

Take a common form of distraction—*noise*.

This is the Age of Noise. We live on a battlefield bombarded by ballyhoo and blab. Silence has become so strange that it frightens. Distraction is the frantically sought god. Wherever we go we see people filling their ears and minds with one loud blast after another. Even at a sports event, you see someone cheering, bending to catch an announcement, lost in the roar of the crowd —all the while eagerly pressing a transistor radio to the ear!

No wonder we don't hear the truth that sets us free.

Trying to solve our problems by distracting ourselves with noise is like trying to untangle traffic by honking the horn.

But there is a way out. We can become aware of all the nerve-wracking noises. We can see how they distract us from finding the True Self. If we discover that a particular mental noise is of our own making, we have power to stop. If it comes from the blaring outer world, we can gradually cease to listen. This restores our natural perception of reality; we begin to see things as they *are*, not as a clamoring world *claims* them to be. For instance, you will discover that the lack of noise, that an inner quietness, is not, as you first supposed, a state of frightening emptiness.

It is just the opposite. It is new beauty. It is much as if you stand in a park, halfway between two orchestras, one playing a lovely symphony, while the other clatters out a jarring racket.

As you turn from the racket, as you deliberately walk away, the atmosphere is more and more filled with the symphony that you barely heard at first.

This idea of inner silence is not philosophical. It is not sentimental. It is not idealistic. It is real. It is a fact. It is something you can use right now.

Dare to Trust Yourself!

Your True Self knows the answer to every problem. When we are inwardly quiet, when we are ready to receive, it speaks. It cannot talk while we are talking. Nor can we hear it whenever we are listening to false counsel. Remember, *your* problem requires *your* answer. No one else's prefabricated solution will clear your mind. Although you must solve it, be cheered by the truth that you *can* solve it. It makes no difference whether the difficulty relates to business affairs or the making of a personal decision or whatever. The True Self, when allowed to speak, tells you what to do.

Look at it like this: Suppose you have a problem in deciding on a new piece of furniture for your living room. The first thing you would *not* do is to turn on the television set, nor would you chat with your neighbors about politics. You would see that these pointless distractions have nothing to do with your problem. What *would* you do? You would retire from noise and distraction. You would sit down and quietly consider the problem. Then, in that state of relaxed receptivity, you would see clearly. The answer comes. You understand just what new furniture would make the room look better. Your own quietness permitted the answer to arrive.

We must learn not to fight a problem, not to resist. We must see that a problem cannot be solved on its own level. A new and higher self is needed. The True Self oversees every complexity, just as the control tower of an airport oversees and guides aircraft on the field.

Dr. Kenneth Walker describes this state of receptivity:

> It is at this moment of inner quietness, of newly revealed freedom, of heightened being, that something of a much more real nature makes its presence felt Perhaps we have been seeking truth all our lives, or else asking to be led to

*it by some teacher whom we believe to know more than we
do, but we have never succeeded in finding what we sought.
And now at this quiet moment, because we are ready for
truth, and have transcended that which has hitherto stood
between truth and us—truth comes to us uninvited, con-
ferring on us also happiness with its magic touch.*[1]

How to Rise Above Any Problem

You are as intelligent as anyone on earth. It is not basic intelligence that is needed; it is the mind's release from its limited
concepts that liberates us from difficulties. Never doubt your
intelligence, but always question its level of awareness.

To get rid of a problem—*any* problem—we must rise above
it, see it in a new way. To illustrate, imagine yourself on a
riverbank, trying to choose a safe passage to the other side.
Because you cannot see hidden dangers, such as swift currents
and jagged rocks, you fear them. You painfully believe that
you must make a risky decision, you conclude that any choice
threatens disaster. Then you wake up. You climb a nearby
tree and once more survey the river. What a difference! From
that higher position you can see beneath the surface; the conditions are clear. Now, is a painful choice still necessary? No!
The need to choose has vanished. You know exactly what to
do. The very act of seeing everything from a superior viewpoint provides total safety. [MENTAL PICTURE 85]

If you only realize the significance of this! What a wonder your
life would be. Painful choice, fearful choice, tormented choice
would vanish forever. In its place you would *know*.

We attain this high level of all-seeing by dropping the burdens
of stubborn viewpoints and false prides. Thus relieved, we climb
to where nothing is a danger, where no one is a threat. *We know
what we are doing.*

Read this inspiring statement from a parent who rose above
domestic problems:

*If you want to be a hero, you have the perfect oppor-
tunity in your own home. Work on yourself, not on your*

---

[1] Kenneth Walker, *A Study of Gurdjieff's Teaching* (London, England: Jonathan
Cape Limited).

family. Awaken yourself, find the wisdom and strength residing in the inner self. Have the heroism to break the negative pattern that is passed from one generation to the next. Make sure that your children are not raised in an atmosphere of fear and hostility. If this was your childhood atmosphere, refuse to pass it on. If you really love your children, no gift is more loving. Do you want your children to love you? Provide them with the inner capacity to do so. Work on yourself and everything else will take care of itself.

How to Avoid Repeated Mistakes

Let's examine a strange feature of human behavior, that of *repeated mistakes*. Have you ever considered how peculiar it is that a man will time and again do the very thing that brings him grief? I am speaking not only of the chronic criminal and the habitual alcoholic, but of everyone who repeats self-defeating actions, like quarreling, doing sloppy work, making cruel remarks to others.

These habits, and hundreds like them, are nothing more than personal mistakes. Why? They harm the individual doing them, plus everyone within his radius. Negative in cause, they produce negative effects.

Why, then—it seems incredible to even ask—does an individual repeat and repeat the same self-harming mistake?

The answer is both simple and complex: *because he is unaware of a better way of behaving.* He does not really see that lawfulness is better for him than lawbreaking, he fails to realize that good work does more for him than sloppy work or that love, not hate, returns a reward. *He does not know how to make himself happy.*

The solution? The *only* solution? We have covered it many times in this book: He must suspect, he must begin to suspect that there is an entirely superior way to live his life. The superior way exists, but first he must suspect that it does, then strike out for it.

Picture a mountain hiker caught in a storm. Assuming that the only shelter is a nearby tree, he huddles beneath it. Hoping to do better, he races to a second tree, and then a third, but none protect him. The idea occurs that there might be a nearby cave, so he runs out and finds one. The cave is a bit better than a tree, but it is still dark and damp. He seeks other caves, but each is as miserable as another. Looking afar, he

sights a distant light. It leads him to a ranger's cabin, where
he finds safety and comfort. He then realizes that he could
have chosen the cabin in the first place, but anxiety and confusion blurred his vision. He philosophically reminds himself,
"Never assume that what you *see* at the moment is all that
there *is*." [MENTAL PICTURE 86]

The spiritual law reads: Let a man catch a glimpse of the better
state and he will take it every time. Inferior habits fall away as
the superior is revealed.

A woman once asked me, "My problem is the feeling of being
cheated. Everyone seems to have more than I. I'm not as young
as I used to be. I've hoped for years that something better would
turn up, that I'd get what I want, that things would be easier.
Nothing has turned up, everything is harder. Perhaps this bitterness is my mistake. You are right on one point—my resentment
is a painful habit. Do you really know how I feel about this?"

Her problem is shared by millions, though most people are not
nearly as frank as she is. They pretend they don't have it. Her
bitterness is a mistake based on the false assumption that getting
this wealth or that husband or this prestige will satisfy her. They
won't. They can't. Nothing demanded by the False Self can satisfy.
Grasp this, and you will never be bothered by this painful habit.

Let me go even deeper than this, though you will find it difficult to accept at the present time. You have never been cheated
out of anything. Never. Please follow this. Your desires for this
or that were based on illusions. You have falsely assumed that
great wealth would anchor you. The fact is, it would only be a
passing excitement, a temporary gratification to the False Self.
You have also believed that prestige or popularity would satisfy.
They won't. They only make you hungry for *more* prestige.
See that these desires are based on false assumptions. Then you
will also see that you have never really been cheated out of anything. Your awareness dissolves bitterness completely. Human
beings are strange. We scream when we are cheated out of poison.

How to Stop Feeling Unwanted

In this section we will take up an internal problem that causes
daily suffering. It is usually so deeply hidden that the sufferer
is unaware of its hold upon him. It is the problem of feeling dis-

approved of, rejected, unwanted, ignored. Few inner states cause more anxiety and confusion. Moreover, because it is a negative state, it manufactures other negativities in the sufferer, including resentment and irritability. Like a faulty alarm clock, such a person is liable to go off anytime.

What is the root of feeling rejected? It is the false premise that you must be this or that kind of person, that you must be popular, wise, attractive, or educated. Nonsense. You don't have to be anything at all. The happiest people in the world are those who don't try to be anything at all. Instead of trying to live, they simply live.

Do you feel the disapproval of others? Let me ask you something. If you didn't feel disapproved of, *where would the disapproval exist?* Stop and think. Where would it exist? It wouldn't. It couldn't. Perhaps you say, "But it exists in the other person's attitude toward me." Again let me ask, "What has *his* attitude to do with *your* feelings?" It has nothing to do with them. Only if you permit it. Once you really see this, you won't permit it. And you will never again feel this disapproval. No one has power to hurt you.

Do not label feelings the way they seem to be. You must not accept a feeling as a fact. Do not react, "I feel rejected," but rather, "A feeling has passed through me which I do not label in any way at all." Do not call the feeling by the name it *seems* to bear. This withdraws false power from the feeling and maintains your peace. Try it.

You are approved for the simple reason that there is really no one to disapprove of you. Try to see the depth of this principle. In reality, there is no disapproval. Other people may make remarks that the False Self *interprets* as disapproval, but they have no power to hurt the person living with his True Self.

People are like a man in a recent television show who read halfway through a mystery novel and then mislaid the book. The suspense drove him to a frantic search through a dozen bookstores and libraries, but without results. In despair, he sank into the sofa in his living room. His eye caught sight of the book poking out from behind a lamp. He solved the mystery by locating the book that had been in his home all the time. [MENTAL PICTURE 87]

So it is with a problem that now seems unsolvable. By living with truthful principles you can clear mysteries, ease tensions, including that of feeling disapproved.

Students of Psycho-Pictography must study its principles persistently. In classes around my home in Los Angeles we have found no rule more valuable. When people don't know the right things to do, they stumble with wrong things. Perseverance teaches right things.

Picture a tall stack of timber and straw set in a clearing of an Indian camp. The stack will be set on fire to signal the start of an Indian festival. Standing at a distance from the stack is an Indian warrior with bow and arrow. One by one he shoots flaming arrows at the stack. Some miss, others fall short. But he keeps shooting. Finally, a flaming arrow strikes the target, setting it ablaze. Soon, the whole camp is bright with warm light. [MENTAL PICTURE 88]

That is how endurance works for us. For a while, nothing happens. We miss and fall short. But we refuse to quit; we insist upon the enlightening truth. So, suddenly, often unexpectedly, we hit the target. We receive light upon areas previously dark to our understanding.

The real hero keeps going, for, "The characteristic of heroism is its persistency." (Emerson)

How to Write Your Own Declaration of Independence

Listen!

Here is a message of cheer for you, whoever you may be and however deep your despair.

There is a way to genuine peace and happiness. There is no need to be anxious over anything. Freedom is yours for the finding. There *is* a way out and you can find it.

What must you do? You must start your search. You need not start skillfully, and you need not be afraid of confusion. Simply start wherever you are. Remember, you are seeking to unfold the Truth that is already hidden within *yourself*. That is where you must look. Let no person and no circumstance hinder your search. It is *your* life!

In all kindness, I must tell you something. You must be willing to give up all forms of pretense. You must especially stop the painful pretense that you already know the answers. The answers to which you cling so desperately—what have they given you besides secret misery? Be humble. Be as a little child. Be willing to receive. Learn to distinguish between truth and illusion. Cast off the old and invite the new.

What must you do? Reclaim your individual integrity. Make your personal declaration of independence.

Do not be afraid to observe yourself constantly and honestly. And do not be afraid of whatever you may see within yourself. Do not run away from it and do not call it by another name. Do not feel guilty and do not condemn yourself. Such attitudes have absolutely no place in your life; they chain you to illusion.

Your honest self-insight is bright light that dispels darkness. Remember, the Truth which you may now so fiercely resist is the very Truth that sets you free. Then, your secret sorrow becomes open joy.

The way out is a great challenge. So march forward, not with gloom and apprehension, but with cheery spirit. You are entering the greatest adventure in life—the finding of your spiritual identity, the True Self. In that Self is everything which you now yearn for and strive toward.

You are not alone. The Truth, which gradually awakens within you, guides and strengthens your every step.

Start today.

And be of good cheer!

FOR YOUR PROBLEM-FREE LIFE

1. The great solution to all human problems is individual inner transformation.
2. Increase your consciousness, your level of awareness.

3. Problems are cured by facing their cause.
4. Dare to trust yourself! You are quite capable of finding the exact answer you need.
5. Be receptive to the counsel of your inner self.
6. Learn to see a problem from a higher level of understanding. Then, it dissolves before your eyes.
7. No one is the permanent slave of repeated mistakes.
8. Remember—you are approved.
9. The Truth comes to the man or woman who welcomes it. Let Psycho-Pictography guide you.
10. Start your search for the superior life today. And do so cheerfully!

15

Enjoy Future Adventures with Psycho-Pictography

Suppose you are interested in a book telling all about rare and exotic fruits. In its pages you discover interesting facts about the papaya, mango, guava. Furthermore, suppose you want to know how to grow these fruits for your own pleasure and sense of accomplishment. But you realize that you must first learn a few things about these fruits—where to obtain plants, how to cultivate them and so on. So every time you run across a problem in the book, you write a question mark opposite it. Perhaps after your first reading of the book you have around fifty question marks.

You continue to study your book about rare fruits. Your understanding grows. As it does, you erase a question mark, one here and one there. By understanding what you need to understand, you erase the problem from both the page and your mind. Finally, you have no more questions. You are in command of the subject. What you formerly *thought about,* you now *know.* [MENTAL PICTURE 89]

That is what you are doing with this book. You are bringing up questions about the wonderful new life and then finding the answers. You are learning to bring forth rare fruitage in every area of your life, whether personal, social, domestic, or financial.

This chapter is designed especially to help you cultivate a richer harvest. It consists of special adventures in Psycho-Pictography that brighten both your inner and outer life. Let's start with:

Tested Techniques for Extra Benefits

Making the most of Psycho-Pictography might be likened once more to harvesting fruit from a tree. While the goal of everyone might be to collect golden fruit, methods may be varied. One man might climb the tree, another might shake the branches, a third might prefer to use a ladder. You can use any of the following techniques, or a combination of all.

Establish a regular reading program with Psycho-Pictography and other self-development books. The very repetition impresses the mind with self-enriching truth. *"How many a man has dated a new era in his life from the reading of a book! The book exists for us, perchance, which will explain our miracles and reveal new ones."* (Henry David Thoreau)

Have you ever noticed how seldom a person really stops to think about a spiritual truth, to actually reflect and ponder its meaning? Take the New Testament principle, "You shall know the truth and the truth shall set you free." Have you ever asked, "What does it mean? How does it apply to me? How can the truth free me from worry?" The point is, take an idea from Psycho-Pictography and think it through, night and day. Try to see its deeper significance. Apply it personally. Watch your life change!

A war drama on television showed a corporal captured by a pair of soldiers in enemy uniforms. The soldier tried to escape several times but was recaptured. It turned out to be a happy capture for the corporal, for his "enemies" turned out to be members of his own army in disguise. A new truth is sometimes like that. We resist it, only to find later that it is our friend. [MENTAL PICTURE 90]

Do not resist a new idea. Be quietly receptive. Go along with it, even unwillingly at first. Sooner or later, it will reveal itself as your ally.

Join other people in sharing the principles of Psycho-Pictography. Suggestions for forming your own local study group are supplied in a following section.

Special Ideas for Self-Enrichment

Use the following spaces to write down the ideas from this book that impress you. There is a good reason why they inspire you the way they do—they wish to tell you something of significance and value. List an idea in your own words, for instance, "Fear is a result of the way I see things, not in the things themselves, so I must work at clearing my mind." Review these special ideas, reflect upon them. For easy reference, note the page where you met the idea.

1. _____

_____ Page ____

2. _____

_____ Page ____

3. _____

_____ Page ____

4. _____

_____ Page ____

5. _____

_____ Page ____

6. _____

_____ Page ____

7. _____

_____ Page ____

8. _____

_____ Page _____

9. _____

_____ Page _____

10. _____

_____ Page _____

11. _____

_____ Page _____

12. _____

_____ Page _____

13. _____

_____ Page _____

14. _____

_____ Page _____

5. _____

_____ Page _____

Psycho-Pictography Study Groups

Upon the publication of my previous book, *SECRETS OF MENTAL MAGIC,* requests have come for details about study groups. Many classes were formed throughout the nation. This section supplies tested plans for organizing your own Psycho-Pictography Study Group.

1. *Meeting place:* Your group can gather in the home of a member or at a church or club. Begin with any convenient location. Later, as the group grows, you can select larger quarters.

2. *Attracting members:* Use all available means for spreading the word about your Psycho-Pictography Study Group. You can inform friends, neighbors, business associates. Use the established methods of publicity, for example: notice in local newspaper, telephone contacts, notice on bulletin boards, mailed invitations, announcements at church or club meetings.

3. *Schedule of meetings:* Weekly meetings at 8 p.m. suit the convenience of most people. Time and frequency of meetings can be adjusted as is best for your particular group.

4. *The program:* In my own Los Angeles study group I give a talk lasting from 30 to 40 minutes. It is followed by a question-and-answer session, which then leads to an open discussion. Light refreshments are usually served while the discussion continues. This is a good basic plan for most study groups.

For Teachers and Leaders

This section supplies practical ideas for anyone who organizes a group for the study of Truth as presented by Psycho-Pictography. The plans may be used by psychologists, clergymen, and other teachers. They are also of value to those who wish to help members of the family or friends to understand the way to personal happiness.

It is always a good idea to give students an active assignment, some adventure in self-discovery that is neither too easy nor too difficult. They might be asked to reflect upon the **Four Golden Keys** (in Chapter 1) or to read a particular Mental Picture in the book.

In keeping with the basic idea of Psycho-Pictography, supply your audience with helpful Mental Pictures, that is, devise your own illustrations and examples. Suppose a class member has difficulty in seeing that a problem is of his own making, that his exterior difficulties are caused by his own mental confusions. You might explain, "It is like a man wanting to hear the beautiful music of a symphony orchestra, but who, at the same time, bangs a sack of tin cans against the wall. He wonders why he can't hear the music!" [MENTAL PICTURE 91]

You might follow up your illustration with a practical technique for your student, like this: "Turn away from your noisy mind. You need not listen to its clamor. You are not a slave to your thoughts."

As a teacher, remember that many people will persistently resist the very Truth that could set them free. The False Self, with all its defenses and vanities, will fight fiercely all attempts to dethrone it. A person controlled by his False Self will often argue and contradict in an effort to protect his false position. As teachers, we must remember that behind these fierce attacks is a suffering individual, one who really knows no other action to take, one who does not know who he is or what he is doing. We must not see him as an offensive person, but as a frightened human being. Our own patience and understanding will help him more than anything else to find his True Self.

Another valuable adventure is to request students to bring questions to class for group discussion. The question may be one foremost in the mind of the student, for example, "How can suffering be turned to insight that dissolves the very suffering?" or "Why does Psycho-Pictography emphasize self-honesty as a power for self-discovery?"

Informative discussions may also be based on a section from the book. The leader reads the section aloud, then asks the audience for comments and questions.

Remember the constant need for cheerful encouragement. Students need reassurance that they are on the right track and that their persistent studies will carry them home at last. It is helpful to sprinkle your lectures with inspiring thoughts, for instance, "No person and no condition really has power to make you feel bad. The false reaction of your mind is what makes you feel bad. But you can learn to react in an entirely new way. You can withdraw the false power from people and circumstances. Inwardly, you are free from feeling bad about anything. Your persistent studies of Psycho-Pictography will more and more reveal this delightful truth to you. Declare your freedom. It is so."

Make the Most of Mental Pictures

The central feature of this book, the Mental Picture, is a tested technique used by the great philosophers and religious teachers to convey Truth. Your guidance and inspiration comes from examples and illustrations which we call Mental Pictures.

Make the most of them with these plans:

Memorize the Mental Pictures that have special meaning to you. To aid your memory, select a key word or phrase that reminds you of a particular one, for instance, "Village Bell" is enough to recall Mental Picture 1.

If a Mental Picture has special value to you, opportunity may arise for you to helpfully pass it on to others. Parents can certainly provide long-lasting mental health to their children by relating these illustrations of Truth. Years later, when guidance is needed, the subconscious may push up to the mind's surface the exact idea needed to avoid a difficulty or solve a problem. Some of the Mental Pictures of special value for young people are 1, 5, 10, 23, 30, 45, 53, 60, 64, 94.

You will find it an interesting adventure to think up a few Mental Pictures of your own. Try it. Keep your eyes and ears open to everything that goes on about you. You will be pleasantly surprised to see how examples and illustrations occur to you. For instance, you may be watching a travelogue on television about Egypt. You would learn that for hundreds of years the Nile River has overflowed its banks, in apparent destruction, but leaving behind a layer of rich soil that sustains life. [MENTAL PICTURE 92]

That is a superb illustration of how suffering, when properly used, can leave us with unexpected spiritual riches.

Finally, remember the dynamic force of a Mental Picture. It is a practical power by which a life-changing truth may be heard, remembered and activated within you. Like a seed, it grows effortlessly into fruitage.

Dr. David Seabury adds this ringing declaration:

> . . . we know today that if you make dynamic designs in your mind of how you wish to behave, your will, like an invincible current, pours into the patterns you have created and gives you a magnetic vigor for the fulfillment of your desires. The will obeys the thought patterns or mental images in your mind and operates as they command.[1]

Mental Pictures of Special Value

Use the following spaces for listing the number and location of Mental Pictures of special value to you. Also, list those you wish to discuss at a Psycho-Pictography Study Group.

---

[1] David Seabury, *The Art of Living Without Tension* (New York: Harper and Row, Publishers, Incorporated, 1958).

1. Mental Picture ____   Page ____
2. Mental Picture ____   Page ____
3. Mental Picture ____   Page ____
4. Mental Picture ____   Page ____
5. Mental Picture ____   Page ____
6. Mental Picture ____   Page ____
7. Mental Picture ____   Page ____
8. Mental Picture ____   Page ____
9. Mental Picture ____   Page ____
10. Mental Picture ____   Page ____
11. Mental Picture ____   Page ____
12. Mental Picture ____   Page ____
13. Mental Picture ____   Page ____
14. Mental Picture ____   Page ____
15. Mental Picture ____   Page ____

Answering Personal Questions

"What do you consider to be the very heart of your teachings?"

The Four Golden Keys supplied in Chapter 1 of Psycho-Pictography.

"How long did it take you to reach inner freedom?"

The question is asked because you want to know how long it will take you. Don't concern yourself with this question. Keep walking ahead.

"What are the rules for becoming a student of Psycho-Pictography?"

None. Students of Psycho-Pictography may come or go as they please. I have no authority over you, nor do I want any. The Truth within you is the only legitimate authority.

"What mental blocks do you see in people that keeps them enslaved?"

Refusal to see themselves as the cause of their own griefs. It's like jumping deliberately into the ocean and then blaming the water for their wetness.

"Will our studies help with problems connected with sex?"

The problem is not sex in itself; it is your enslaving thoughts about it. One tormenting thought is that you are being cheated of its pleasures. Yes, these studies clear your mind.

"You seem to be free of negative emotions, so tell me, what is it like to be inwardly at ease?"

It cannot be explained with words. Work with yourself and you will know for yourself. This isn't an evasion of your question; it's the only answer.

"What technique for self-discovery have you found of personal value?"

Self-observation, that is, an alert awareness of every thought and feeling as it comes and goes.

"Is *Psycho-Pictography* your original idea?"

The idea of a book centered around Mental Pictures is original with me, but the Truth conveyed by them is universal.

"Do you worry or feel resentful?"

If I told you no, would you believe me? You will know whether I live without worry only when you are able to do so. You cannot accept as a fact anything that is above your personal level of experience.

"What negative emotions do you find that people like least to admit?"

Feelings of injustice, self-pity, the idea that life never rewards one as he so rightfully deserves. They are cunningly hidden from the self—and do terrible damage.

"Why do you insist that we work for personal profit in our spiritual life, rather than working to help others?"

Because it prevents hypocrisy. You must first find your own True Self before you can really help others.

"How can we tell whether a certain teacher or book is speaking from the Truth and not from mere opinion?"

Work at finding the Truth within yourself. At a certain point in your development you will see clearly whether a teacher is speaking from a level of spiritual awareness or from the lower level of a conditioned mind.

"If I came to you for encouragement, what would you say?"

You need not be trapped. Desperate desires can be dissolved. You need not fear anything whatsoever. There is abundant supply for all your genuine needs. Place the Truth above all else and all else will be added to you. Mental struggle is unnecessary. Dare to relax. Be aware. Let the Truth set you free.

Psycho-Pictography Points to Ponder

Wisdom is a state characterized not by knowing what you want, but by realizing what you don't need.

Don't be afraid to let life just happen.

A decrease in misfortune begins the same day you sincerely decide to work on your inner self.

Whenever you are troubled by anything at all, say, "This merely represents something I don't understand." Then, drop it. If necessary, repeat it a dozen times a day. I assure you that you are on the right track.

A man's level of spiritual maturity can be tested by the amount of truth he can take without getting angry or upset.

Opinions spring from the False Self and cause pain. Certainty is part of the True Self and insures peace.

Fearful thoughts? Stand back and observe them playing around, just as you would watch with amusement as mischievous children try to scare you with Halloween masks.

A chief enemy of genuine happiness is the frantic manufacturing of artificial activities that give the illusion of happiness.

When you are *consciously* sick and tired of the way you are living, there is hope. Unconscious despair is a refusal to face the facts. *Conscious* suffering is heroism.

A person fiercely resists the Truth that could liberate him because he falsely fears that there is nothing else beyond his illusions. But there is.

When you no longer need to prove your intelligence, you have it.

Try to meet a problem as if you have no thoughts at all toward it. This prevents rigid and unworkable ideas from operating and provides entrance for a higher level of understanding. A problem is really solved only when it is thoroughly understood.

Don't assume. Find the fact.

You must constantly ask yourself whether the ideas and plans by which you live are really making you happy. This courageous and honest inquiry can bring the dawn of new life, for it indicates your willingness to abandon the False Self for the True Self.

Are you consenting to inner transformation?

See the difference between dreaming your life and living your dream.

You cannot fly higher than your own level of awareness. To state it in positive fashion, you achieve higher levels of tranquility as you reach loftier heights of self-awareness. Awareness *is* tranquility.

You are growing in understanding when you don't mind when nothing exciting happens to you.

We always lose when we argue with the Truth.

By refusing to pretend that we already know the Truth, we finally know it for sure.

We must go beyond the mere quoting to the actual experiencing. "Be anxious for nothing." Are you anxious for nothing, or is this merely a New Testament phrase to which you cling? You can arrive at that state where you are really anxious for nothing.

You will be free of negative emotions as soon as you stop justifying them.

When you don't know what else to do, *try.*

You are not who you think you are. A false sense of identity, rooted in fear and illusion, causes pain. You are not your False Self. You are your True Self.

Picture a man standing on the first floor of a building while listening to a man speaking from the fifth floor. There can be no communication nor understanding. There is a mental level, useful for worldly affairs, and there is a spiritual level, necessary for understanding higher happiness. You can ascend to it. [MENTAL PICTURE 93]

You Were Made to Conquer!

The ancient Greek myth about Thesus and the magic ball of thread supplies an effective Mental Picture. King Minos of Crete constructed a hugh labyrinth beneath his castle. It was a dark and complex maze of corridors and false trails. An enemy tossed into the labyrinth was hopelessly lost. Even worse, King Minos imprisoned the Minotaur, a monster, half bull and half man, in the heart of the underground dungeon.

Thesus, a young prince from another land, was scheduled to be sacrificed to the Minotaur. He was imprisoned in a cell, ready to be led to the labyrinth and abandoned to his cruel fate.

But Ariadne, the beautiful daughter of King Minos, fell in love with the dashing Thesus. She vowed to save him from the dreadful plot. At midnight, she crept to the cell of Thesus and gave him a magic ball of thread. Assuring him that guidance and protection were now his, she helped him escape his cell.

Thesus slipped through the darkness to the entrance of the labyrinth. He tossed the magic ball of thread to the ground, then followed along as it rolled its way down dark passages and around sharp bends. Finally, the young hero came face to face with the roaring Minotaur. They battled, and soon, the monster was no more. Thesus followed the magic thread back through the labyrinth to Ariadne and to freedom. [MENTAL PICTURE 94]

That is how the Truth directs the man who really wants to find the way. No matter how dark the passage or how confused the mind, regardless of monsters encountered, the magical thread of Truth is there to guide and protect. It will fight for the man when he faces the monsters he must conquer, that is, his own subconscious illusions and repressed fears. Every heroic adventurer will sooner or later find himself with the needed courage, strength, and wisdom.

You are not alone.

And you were made to conquer.

ABOUT THE AUTHOR

Vernon Howard richly deserves his fame as an author and lecturer. His inspiring books enjoy a world-wide circulation of 2 million copies, and the figure climbs yearly. They are used in psychological clinics, colleges, churches, and in the homes of men and women who want a richer life. His previous book, *SECRETS OF MENTAL MAGIC,* has attracted new and enthusiastic circles of readers.

He is a unique teacher and lecturer. His dynamic purpose is to supply each member of his audience with self-liberating insight. "It is always the Truth," he reminds, "that sets you free."

Vernon Howard lives in the Highland Park section of Los Angeles where he conducts classes, including Psycho-Pictography Study Groups.